Joachim Mayer

Balcony &
Container
Plants

from A to Z

➤ Popular plants for lush, dreamy balcony
  gardens
➤ The best ideas for every time of year

Contents

Choosing Plants

Plant Profiles

Designing with Plants

Appendix

Choosing Plants

There are many beautiful balcony and container plants available. Take plenty of time to make a well-thought-out, careful selection—that's the best guarantee for gorgeous plants that will give you year-round enjoyment.

On Offer: Immense Variety

The extensive profile section of this book covers over 200 plants, with short descriptions and tips on care. There are many species, among which you are sure to find something beautiful and suitable for your balcony or patio. But no selection, however large, can truly cover everything that can be grown in planters. Newly introduced "exotics" constantly enlarge the assortment, as do robust garden plants in compact forms for growing in pots.

This book provides an overview of the plant groups that basically make good candidates for your "green living room."

Balcony Plants

Balcony plants include all the plants that embellish balcony flowerboxes, bowls, pots, and hanging planters and usually can be combined with other species in the same container. We distinguish among them on the basis of botanical classification, use, growth habits, and developmental features:

➤ **Annual flowers:** By far the largest group, annual flowers include the petunia, Livingstone daisy, and nemesia hybrids. They are grown from seed in early spring and are usually planted starting in mid-May and, from early summer on, provide a constant supply of flowers until fall. When they die, they must be grown again from seed and/or planted the next year. In warmer climates, they may grow as perennials, herbaceous plants, or even shrubs, but in North America wintering over annuals

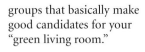

Bulb flowers like those of the genus *Narcissus* will supply glorious flowers in spring.

Special Plant Wishes
Even though garden stores and garden centers often have quite a wide selection of plants, they certainly aren't able to keep everything in stock. If you are interested in a particular variety, you should start studying gardening magazines with greater care in March and April. There you will find up-to-date sources of supply, even for unusual plants. Many mail-order plant suppliers and specialized garden stores also present their offerings on the Internet.

is rarely worthwhile.

➤ **Annual climbers:** These annuals also include species with long, twining or creeping shoots, such as the cup and saucer vine. Because they grow rapidly, most can be used as a decorative screen.

➤ **Biennial flowers:** Sown in summer, biennials produce only leaves until fall and do not flower until the following spring. Such species, including English daisies and forget-me-nots, go well with spring bulb flowers.

➤ **Bulbous and tuberous flowers:** Plants that sprout from bulbs or tubers, such as tulips and narcissus, are primarily spring bloomers. You can pot the bulbs in the fall,

take on the role of the balcony flowers in fall and winter. If you grow them for several years, you must repot these plants in individual containers over time when they get larger and treat them as potted woody plants.

Container Plants and Potted Woody Plants

Container plants lend an exotic flair to your balcony or patio.

Many of the plants you will grow in large pots and tubs will stay with you for years. For this reason, you need to choose them with special care.

➤ **Container plants** are usually woody plants from warmer countries. In some more northern areas, they can't be put outside until mid-May and must be brought to a well-protected winter location, before fall's first frost.

but it is easier to buy plants in early spring and then pot them. In planters, tuberous and bulbous flowers, which are actually perennials, are usually grown only until they stop flowering; then they are replaced by new ones the next year.

➤ **Herbaceous perennials:** These long-lasting, non-woody plants can frequently be grown in containers for many years. They are available in a wide range of plants, including shade-tolerant species such as astilbe and species that bloom either in early spring or late in the year.

➤ **Dwarf woody plants:** Young dwarf conifers and small evergreen deciduous plants with ornamental fruit

➤ **Potted woody plants** are shrubs, trees, woody climbers, or semishrubs that, unlike exotic container plants, can be grown outdoors in almost all climates year-round. Since they are more or less frost-hardy, they often can be wintered over outdoors.

Fruits, Vegetables, Herbs
Fresh, tasty foods straight

from the balcony box or container is a good thing. Keep in mind, however, that almost all useful plants need lots of sun and very regular care, if you want to have something to harvest.

➤ **Fruits:** Here the palette ranges from strawberries to small apple trees to kiwi trees in tubs. Small forms of most fruit species are also available for growing in pots. Nevertheless, over time, fruit-bearing woody plants will need quite a lot of room.

A little place can be found almost anywhere for herbs and bush tomatoes.

➤ **Vegetables:** Balcony tomatoes are the most popular container vegetable, but all kinds of vegetables, from radishes to zucchini, can be grown in planters.

➤ **Herbs:** Planted in containers, herbs are harvested in ample quantities but require little space. In addition, their often aromatic scents are especially good for balconies and patios.

The Right Choice

> **Hydrangeas, hostas, and boxwood are quite shade-tolerant.**

When selecting a plant, your preferences are of primary importance. As part of this process, give some thought to the design and overall effect as well (→ page 233). If the plants are to remain a source of real pleasure over the long run, however, the site conditions on your balcony or patio must provide a suitable environment. Therefore, when choosing plants, be sure to consider the various light require-ments and the special sensi-tivity of some species to weather factors such as wind and rain.

Light and Sun

To thrive, all plants need light and warmth, but their requirements may vary sig-nificantly, depending on origin and natural habitat. Depending on their need for light, plants are divided into three categories, which

"Southerners" like the oleander usually like sunny locations.

are often designated by symbols (→ pages 26, 27, and inside front cover):

➤ Plants for sunny, bright locations. Many plants enjoy some shade at midday instead of sitting in the blazing sun all day long.

➤ Plants for partial shade, that is, for places that get no sun for about half the day or have light shade for many hours at a time.

➤ Plants for shady locations, where there is direct sunlight for a few hours at most.

The amount of sunlight that reaches your balcony or patio is determined primarily by the direction it faces. Direct sun, as a basic princi-ple, diminishes from south through west and east to north. But neighboring buildings, roofs, and the like can heavily influence the light conditions. For this reason, general recommendations such as "for a balcony facing south," "for a balcony facing west," and so forth are somewhat problematic. Only you can tell from your own observation how the light conditions in your "green living room" should be rated.

EXTRA TIP

Often some shade is tolerated

In the plant profiles, you can see that many species tolerate both full sun and partial shade. But even strictly sun-loving plants often will still thrive in lightly shaded spots, though they usually bloom less profusely there. The same applies to partial-shade plants that are growing in the shade. Because plants are more concerned with light, which they need for photosynthesis, than with sunshine, plants that tolerate partial shade also do quite well on bright balconies with a northern exposure.

tive plants—such as geraniums, wax begonias, blue marguerites, and Apache beggarticks—work best.

Modern trailing petunia cultivars can brave wind and weather.

Rain and Wind

What falls from the sky admittedly will keep you from having to water, but steady rainfall will affect the blooms of many species and may also cause the soil to become waterlogged. Completely unprotected places, especially if they face west, are therefore somewhat problematic for species that are sensitive to rain and damp. In case of doubt, purchase weatherproof species like modern hanging petunias, single geraniums, gold coins, and marigolds. Wind can seriously stress the plants and make them look disheveled. In unprotected west-facing sites, as well as on high-rise and rooftop balconies, nonsensi-

Other Selection Criteria

➤ **Space requirements:** Always keep the plants' subsequent size in mind—especially with container plants and woody plants in pots, which often grow tall and wide over time. Plants that are placed or planted too close together will soon get in each other's way, in terms of both growth and visual effect. In addition, comfort and mobility are limited when an area is almost completely filled with plants.

➤ **Places for wintering over:** Most container plants and sensitive woody plants in pots need frost-free, but cool and bright winter quarters (→ Profiles, starting on page 124), so you should keep this in mind when planning your garden.

➤ **Load-bearing capacity of the balcony:** Large plants in heavy tubs with damp soil can weigh a lot. In addition, you may have solidly built

furniture and heavy floor coverings that add to the load on the balcony structure. Make sure to stay below the maximum limit permitted by local regulations; if in doubt, consult a civil engineer.

➤ **Poisonous plants:** Some of the plants designated as poisonous in the profile section can cause allergic skin reactions. If you are sensitive in this regard, you should select less toxic species, or at least wear gloves when dealing with

For warmth-loving container plants, a conservatory is ideal.

them. If there are small children in your home, you should avoid poisonous plants and plants with spines or thorns.

Where to buy?

The best source for plants is specialized dealers in the horticultural industry— nurseries, well-run garden centers, or flower shops. Generally, they guarantee optimal care all the way from cultivation to sale and provide expert advice. Often you will find an especially wide selection, including unusual plants, from mail-order gardening companies (→ also Extra Tip, page 7). Admittedly, with the mail-order suppliers, you can examine the merchandise only after delivery, but in general most gardeners are pleased with the experience. Basically, there is nothing against occasionally buying young plants at the supermarket or do-it-yourself store, where quite inexpensive, often completely acceptable plants are available for every balcony season. However, you need to take an especially close look at these plants before you buy.

Give shipments of plants a thorough inspection immediately upon arrival.

Lebende Pflanzen

When to Buy?

Buying **plants for the balcony** is a seasonal matter, though the focus, of course, is on the glories of summer. The peak seasons of availability are February/March for spring planting, April/May for summer planting, and September/October for fall and winter planting.

In general, you will find the largest selection at the beginning of each of these sales seasons. Some nurseries and garden centers sell specimens that bloom especially early, and this naturally arouses buyers' interest. Because such plants are frequently forced, with great effort, in heated greenhouses, gardeners are frequently disappointed in their growth on balconies and patios, because these plants are not robust enough or because the early blooming period ends early as well. The warmth-loving **container or tub plants** should not come outdoors until mid-May or even late May. This is also a good time to buy them; then the new beauties have time to settle in on your balcony or patio until fall. **Potted woody**

plants and herbaceous perennials cultivated in containers can usually be placed in their final planters in March and April and put outdoors; however, that can also be done during the summer.

> **When the plants are so charmingly presented, shopping is a pleasure.**

Checking the Plants
The healthier and more vigorous the plants seem when purchased, the more likely it is that you will be able to enjoy them for a long time. For this reason, you need to examine the plants thoroughly. Here are the important points to check:

EXTRA TIP

Watch out when planting early
In many parts of the country, if you buy summer plants as early as April and put them outdoors, cool temperatures or even late spells of frost can harm them even in May. Therefore, the traditional planting date, from mid-May on (after the spring frosts), has stood the test of time. Boxes that have been planted early should be brought indoors during cold spells and placed in a bright, cool location. If need be, you can also cover the plants with plastic film or nonwoven fleece, available in garden stores.

15

Choosing Plants

➤ compact growth, with good branching

➤ healthy leaves with good overall color, with no signs of disease or pest infestation (check undersides of leaves, too)

➤ plenty of buds visible on balcony flowers and blooming container/tub plants

➤ well-rooted pot ball, with light-colored roots, full of sap and with no signs of decay

Growing Plants Yourself

Raising balcony flowers from seed on your own does not translate into huge savings because commercially available plants are usually quite inexpensive. But it can be a lot of fun to raise the little plants yourself and watch then grow. Besides,

Using several planters made of the same material creates a harmonious effect.

Young plants are best hardened off in a sheltered spot.

often certain species or cultivars that are hard to find as young plants can be obtained only by cultivating them yourself.

For starting plants from seed, beginning in early spring, you need a warm, bright spot. Usually a window sill is a good choice for this—if possible, however, not next to a south-facing window directly in the blazing sun because the seedlings and young plants do not tolerate such conditions well.

Shallow bowls or flats fitted with an appropriate cover are quite practical. It will not only provide warmth but ensure the necessary level of atmospheric humidity. Always use special potting mix, and preferably use high-quality seeds.

Suitable Planters

The process of acquiring plants for balconies and patios is not over until you have appropriate planters and good soil—both are essential requirements for healthy growth. Decorative tubs, pots, bowls, and other receptacles can accentuate the plants in a special way or can become a design element all on their own. In any event, however, you also need to take the following into account when selecting planters:

➤ **Drainage holes:** Make sure that there are holes on the bottom of the planter through which extra water can run off. They are essential, unless you are trying to grow marsh plants. The holes prevent standing water and root rot. Some planters have prestamped images of drainage holes on the bottom; all you need to do is punch them out. Only some hanging planters are sold without any overflow openings, because dripping water is undesirable. Here, then, you have to use extreme care when watering.

➤ **Planter size:** The planter should suit the size of the plant and its growth habit; it should not be too small. Planters must have enough room for the root ball, as well as a couple of inches free all around so that you can add fresh soil. Appropriate balcony planter boxes are at least 6 in. (15 cm) high and 7 in. (18 cm) wide; for more than one row of plants, 8–10 in. (20–25 cm) is better. Planter bowls must be at least 6 in. (15 cm) deep in the center, with 8 in. (20 cm) even better, so that the roots have enough soil available.

➤ **Weight:** Heavy planters are quite stable but very hard to move; for example, consider carrying tub plants to their winter quarters. Moreover, in choosing heavy

Make sure that hanging planters are stable.

EXTRA TIP

Reservoir planters
Almost all types of planters are available with a reservoir—a practical solution because such receptacles eliminate the need for frequent watering in summer. The planters must be equipped with a water-level indicator and an overflow device. Keep in mind that the containers are quite heavy when the reservoir is full.

containers, you need to consider the load-carrying capacity of balcony railings and floor surfaces (→ page 12). The heaviest planters are made of clay and terracotta, as well as natural or artificial stone. Stone, however, usually is used only for planter troughs that stay in one location.

➤ **Resistance to weather:** Spending more for stable, weatherproof planters usually pays off in terms of greater durability. Planters that hold plants to be wintered over outdoors must be frost-proof.

Soils and Substrates

Spending a few dollars more to get a high-quality potting soil is a good investment. It will retain its advantageous, porous structure for a long time, storing nutrients and water and releasing them again in the right amounts. In addition, it will not get damp as quickly as low-priced soil. High-quality potting soils are especially important for container plants and other perennials, which generally need repotting only every two or three years. Special container-plant soils or all-purpose soils are recommended for this purpose. Various peat-free mixtures now have become available, and they have a good track record with balcony and container

> **Raising plants from seed can turn into a "green passion."**

plants. By using them, you can contribute toward preserving bogs and swamplands. Special potting mixes are recommended for petunias (especially for profusely blooming hanging petunias and trailing petunias), citrus plants, and all highly lime-sensitive plants. The latter should be potted in rhododendron or azalea soil, if no potting soils designed especially for them are available from a garden store.

Technical Terms from A to Z

➤ **acid medium**
Soil with → pH value and lime content.

➤ **annuals**
Plants that die after one growing season, → see also pages 6/7.

➤ **ball**
The soil around the roots, held together by lateral roots and rootlets.

➤ **basal cutting**
Cutting taken from a part of the shoot near the base of the plant.

➤ **bloom**
Blossom, florescence, mass of flowers.

➤ **botanical name**
The scientific plant name is composed of the genus name, which is capitalized (as in *Bidens*) and the species name, which is lowercased (as in *ferulifolia*) (→ also Species, → Genus). The botanical name *Bidens ferulifolia*, for example, denotes, in a way that is internationally understandable and unmistakable, a yellow-flowering plant for which English has many common names, including Apache beggarticks, threadleaf tickseed, bur marigold, and gold Marie.

➤ **clipping**
Trimming with clippers as opposed to fingers.

➤ **container-grown plant**
Young plant grown in the nursery in plastic pots or planter bags. Such plants can be potted at almost any time of year (even while blooming).

➤ **cultivar (cultivated variety)**
Selectively bred population of a → species, for example, with a certain flower color, size, or special growth habit; usually designated by single quotation marks, as in 'Ville de Paris,' a reliable pelargonium cultivar.

➤ **cutting**
Part of the shoot that takes root after being separated from the parent plant and grows into a complete new plant. Take cuttings that are 10–20 cm long, with 4–5 leaves or leaf pairs, and after removing the bottom-most leaf pair, stick them in special starter growing soil.

➤ **deadheading**
Removing dead or dying flowers and leaves.

➤ **deciduous**
Plants that drop their leaves in fall, unlike → evergreens.

➤ **delayed-release fertilizer (slow-release fertilizer)**
Fertilizer that only gradually releases its nutrients, depending on the temperature and the dampness of the potting mix. Ideally, it should be mixed with the soil even before planting. The supply of fertilizer lasts for up to six months.

➤ **division**
Simple method of propagating herbaceous perennials and the like by dividing the root-ball into two or more pieces with several leaves and/or leaf buds and then replanting them.

➤ **double, double-flowering**
Flowers with several circles of petals. Depending on their number, the flowers look semidouble or double and thus particularly luxuriant.

➤ **drainage materials**
Coarse-grained material placed on the bottom of the pot or box, or at least over the drainage holes, to improve water drainage. Good choices are clay pellets (used in hydroculture), clay shards, or gravel.

➤ **evergreen**
Plants that retain their leaves year round, in contrast to → deciduous ones. Some, however, lose their leaves in winter if the conditions are unfavorable (e.g., if wintered over in the dark).

➤ **family**
In the botanical classification of the plant kingdom, a group of → genera with several characteristics in common.

➤ **fertilizing (feeding)**
Supplying with nutrients. It must be done regularly, starting about four weeks after planting. Use only special fertilizers for balcony or container/tub plants, and never exceed the manufacturer's recommended dose. Special fertilizers are advisable for some plants, such as rhododendron food for lime-sensitive species. For all container plants and other candidates for wintering over, stop feeding in early August and start again once new growth begins to appear in the spring.

➤ **genus**
In the botanical classification of the plant kingdom, a group of → species with a number of common characteristics.

➤ **geraniums**
Name in widespread use for members of the genus *Pelargonium*; strictly speaking, it is incorrect. These plants, popular for centuries, were first viewed as a cranesbill species (genus *Geranium*), but since 1789 they have been taxonomically classified as members of the genus *Pelargonium*.

21

➤ **germination temperature**
Range of temperatures at which the seeds germinate best.

➤ **hanging basket**
Receptacle made of woven plastic or wire, which is hung from the ceiling or wall like a → hanging planter. The wire frame structure of the plant baskets leaves room for charming additions on the sides as well. An insert (coconut fiber, moss, plastic, etc.) keeps the soil from trickling out.

➤ **hanging planter**
Planter that can be suspended from the ceiling or hung on the wall, for hanging/trailing plants and others.

➤ **herbaceous perennial**
Plant with a nonwoody stem that lives for more than one growing season, see also page 8.

➤ **hybrid**
Cross between two or more → species, which combines the advantages of the different parents and almost represents a permanent species of its own, such as the *Petunia* hybrids. In addition, there are also crosses of various → cultivars, such as the F_1 hybrids of annual flowers and vegetables.

➤ **light germinator**
Plant species whose seeds germinate only when they are left bare or covered with only a wafer-thin layer of soil at most.

➤ **pH value**
A measure of the acidity of soil or water, which can be determined with indicator sticks, available, for example, from drugstores or specialty stores. A pH value of 7 is neutral, and values below that indicate an acid milieu, while values above 7 (up to 14) signal an alkaline or basic environment. High pH values indicate high lime content—thus lime-sensitive plants such as rhododendrons thrive only in acid potting soil.

➤ **pinching (out, back)**
Nipping or shearing off shoot tips and buds of young plants to promote branching and compact growth; possible even with some older plants.

➤ **pricking (out)**
Transplanting seedlings that have grown some and are too close together; this can be done either singly into small pots or about 2 in. (4–5 cm) apart into new dishes or flats; it is advisable to use only special propagating or starter soil.

➤ **seedling**
Very young plant in the first weeks following germination from a seed.

➤ **semishrub**
Perennial plant whose lower branch parts become woody over time, while the upper ones remain herbaceous, such as pelargonium and lavender.

➤ **series**
Group of similar → cultivars with a common breeding origin.

➤ **single, single-flowering**
Flowers with only one circle of petals surrounding the stamens and pistil.

➤ **softwood cutting**
Slightly woody → cutting, whose bark is not yet completely hard.

➤ **soil**
Mixture of peat, clay, humus, or peat substitutes.

➤ **sowing (growing from seed)**
Sowing seeds in a warm place with later transplanting; also known as cultivation or growing from seed.

➤ **species**
In botany, the "plant as such": Scarlet sage (*Salvia splendens*) and common sage (*Salvia officinalis*), for example, are two different species of the sage → genus sage (*Salvia*).

➤ **standing water**
State in which the soil in the planter is constantly saturated or even oversaturated with water; very dangerous, as the roots as well as bulbs and tubers may soon begin to rot and die.

➤ **stem cutting**
Cutting taken from the midportion of a stem or shoot; also known as shoot cutting.

➤ **succulent**
Plant that can store large amounts of water in thick, fleshy leaves. Examples: agave, crassula.

➤ **tip cuttings**
Cuttings taken from the tips of the main stems or lateral shoots.

➤ **winter protection**
In colder climates, precautions necessary to protect potted woody plants that are outdoors. Of prime importance is insulating the container, by laying Styrofoam under it, wrapping it in burlap or the like, and for heavier frosts also covering the substrate surface with leaves, fir branches, or cardboard.

Plant
Profiles

Subdivided into "balcony plants,"
"container plants," and "tasty
choices," the following pages offer
information and tips on care for
numerous attractive and useful
plants.

Finding Your Way Around

The plants are assigned to three subsections:

➤ **Balcony plants:** These include annual and biennial summer flowers, flowering bulbs and tubers, potted herbaceous perennials, and annual climbers.

➤ **Container plants:** These include winter-hardy potted woody plants and dwarf forms of woody plants, some of which were originally planted in mixed balcony boxes but later are placed singly in planters.

➤ **Tasty choices:** This includes herbs, vegetables, and fruits that can be grown in boxes or pots.

Within these three subdivisions, the plants are arranged alphabetically by their botanical names. The index at the back of the book will help when you want to search under the English common name.

The Plant Profiles

The information next to the photos will give you, at a glance, important data about the plants, including their height, bloom time (for edible plants, harvest time), and an indication of the plant group to which each species belongs. These facts are accompanied by symbols (→ page 27 and the inside front cover) that quickly tell you what you need to know about location, care requirements, and use.

Above the text of each profile, you will see the botanical name that unmistakably identifies the plant, followed by the most common English name. Under the individual headings, which differ slightly from one plant group to another, you will find the following information:

Family: The English (common) and botanical (scientific) names of each plant family.

Description: A brief list of the major characteristics including the flowers, with their principal coloring; the growth habits and properties; the fruit, insofar as it is of interest; and, for species with decorative foliage, the leaves.

Location: More detailed information about light requirements, as well as any possible sensitivity to wind and rain.

Sowing: Time and germination temperatures; only for

annual and biennial summer flowers that are easily grown from seed.

Planting: The planting date and/or the time to move balcony flowers outdoors, as well as the required distances between plants.

Care: The most important steps in plant care and any special needs and chores, including data on the optimal conditions for all plants that can be wintered over.

Propagation: Methods of propagation that can be used. If the word "cuttings" is mentioned here, you should give preference to tip cuttings, but you can also use stem or shoot cuttings (→ Technical Terms from A to Z, beginning on page 20).

Design: Tips and suggestions for accentuating the best features of each plant.

Species/Cultivars: Related species or reliable cultivated varieties.

Only for herbs, vegetables, and fruits:

Cultivation: Summary of the most important facts about sowing seeds and/or planting.

Harvesting: Information on the time of ripeness and harvesting procedures.

Symbols Used in This Book

 The plant likes things bright and largely sunny.

 The plant does best in partial shade.

 The plant will thrive even in shade.

 Water the plant generously (daily in summer).

 Water the plant in moderation (roughly every two to three days, more often in hot weather).

 Water the plant sparingly (don't let the root ball dry out).

 The plant can be used in hanging planters and baskets.

 The plant will climb up poles, trellises, or walls.

 The plant contains toxic substances or skin irritants.

Balcony Plants
from A to Z

Lush flowers from early spring until almost winter, cheerful, colorful balcony boxes, hanging planters of flowers with luxuriantly cascading shoots, opulent blooms, tender beauties, and decorative foliage—with the immense richness and variety of the wide selection of balcony plants, you can help yourself to a majestic abundance of colors and textures.

Height:
*6–10 in.
(15–25 cm)*
Bloom Time:
*May–
October*

*semishrub
grown as an
annual*

Ageratum houstonianum

Ageratum

Other Names: Flossflower
Family: Aster, daisy, or sunflower (Asteraceae)
Description: Flowers in blue, violet, pink, rose, and white; corymbs with rounded flower heads; growth habit broad and bushy, compact
Location: Best in the sun but still thrives in partial shade; wind-resistant; quite rain-tolerant
Sowing: January–March; germination temperature of 64–68 °F (18–20 °C); prick seedlings early
Planting: Beginning in mid-May, 6–8 in. (15–20 cm) apart
Care: Keep evenly damp, avoid standing water; feed every two weeks; remove dead flowers. Can be wintered over in a bright spot at 50–59 °F (10–15 °C), then shorten shoots by one third in spring.
Propagation: By tip cuttings in early spring
Design: Can be combined in numerous ways with other balcony flowers; blue and violet cultivars go especially well with yellow bloomers such as marigolds

Height:
*16–30 in.
(40–75 cm)*
Bloom Time:
*July–
October*

*annual
summer
flower*

Amaranthus caudatus

Love-Lies-Bleeding

Family: Amaranth (Amaranthaceae)
Origin: South America
Description: Red, long, dangling spikes; growth: erect, bushy; large, elongated oval leaves
Location: Full sun, warm
Sowing: March–April; germination temperature of 59–64 °F (15–18 °C); starting in late April, can also be sown directly in planter
Planting: Starting in late May, 12–16 in. (30–40 cm) apart
Care: Keep evenly moist; every two weeks, a low dose of fertilizer and/or low-nitrogen fertilizer; remove faded inflorescences regularly
Design: These plants, which grow quite full in good conditions, do better in large pots than in flowerboxes; good partners are, for example, yellow-flowering, vigorous species like *Asteriscus maritimus* and *Bidens ferulifolia*
Species/Cultivars: The related *A. cruentus* grows only 12–20 in. (30–50 cm) high and has erect inflorescences in shades of red or green

Height:
*4–10 in.
(10–25 cm)*
Bloom Time:
June–October

*herbaceous
perennial
grown as an
annual*

Anagallis monelli

Flaxleaf Pimpernel

Family: Primrose (Primulaceae)
Origin: Mediterranean area, northwestern Africa
Description: Flowers blue, red, saucer-shaped, up to 3/4 in.
(2 cm) in diameter; bushy growth habit, with prostrate to
pendulous shoots
Location: Sunny or partial shade; warm, sheltered
Sowing: February–April; germination temperature of 68 °F
(20 °C); young plants must be pinched back
Planting: Starting in mid-May, 8–10 in. (20–25 cm) apart
Care: Keep moderately damp; feed every three weeks; occa-
sionally deadhead
Design: Very pretty in a hanging planter or basket; in mixed
flowerboxes with yellow, red, or white partners such as
Calceolaria integrifolia and erect geraniums/pelargoniums; do
not combine with extremely vigorous species
Species/Cultivars: 'Skylover' has gentian-blue flowers; 'Sun-
rise,' reddish-orange ones; both varieties have 20-in.-long
(50-cm-long), pendulous shoots

Height:
*6–12 in.
(15–30 cm)*
Bloom Time:
June–October

*herbaceous
perennial
grown as an
annual*

Anthirrinum majus

Snapdragon

Family: Figwort (Scrophulariaceae)
Origin: Southern Europe, North Africa
Description: Flowers yellow, red, orange, pink, white, also bicolored; depending on cultivar, brightly colored or pastel; flowers snap open like tiny "dragon mouths" when lightly pressed; growth habit: bushy to mound-forming; there are also trailing cultivars
Location: Preferably sunny, but partial shade as well
Sowing: Beginning in February; germination temperature of 59–68 °F (15–20 °C), pinch back center shoots of young plants
Planting: From late April/early May, 8 in. (20 cm) apart
Care: Keep moderately damp; feed a low dose of fertilizer every two weeks
Design: Tolerant partner with many color hues, hence very versatile in combinations; especially good with snapdragon color mixtures are blue or white flowers, such as *Lobelia erinus, Nierembergia,* feverfew, blue marguerite, or white geraniums

Height:
6–14 in.
(15–35 cm)
Bloom Time:
September–
October

herbaceous
perennial

Aster-Dumosus Hybrids

Bushy Aster

Family: Aster, daisy, or sunflower (Asteraceae)
Origin: North America
Description: Numerous flowers in white, pink, red, violet, or blue with yellow center; forms compact cushions
Location: Sunny, also light shade
Planting: In August/September, 8–12 in. (20–30 cm) apart
Care: Keep moderately damp; supply with slow-release fertilizer in spring and, if necessary, feed again in summer; can be wintered over in a frost-free, bright place or outdoors with winter protection
Propagation: By division in spring or from cuttings in early summer
Design: Attractive partner for coordinated colors of chrysanthemums, *Sedum* species, heather, and other fall bloomers; blue and violet cultivars are especially good, as these colors otherwise are rare in fall; for flowerbox planting, use low-growing cultivars such as 'Schneekissen' (white)

Height:
*10–12 in.
(25-30 cm)*
Bloom Time:
*April/May–
October*

*herbaceous
perennial
grown as an
annual*

Asteriscus maritimus

Gold Coin

Other Names: Mediterranean beach daisy, golden dollar
Family: Aster, daisy, or sunflower (Asteraceae)
Origin: Mediterranean region, Canary Islands
Description: Flowers golden yellow, similar to small sunflowers; grows broad and quite robust, slightly trailing
Location: Preferably sunny, also flourishes in places with blazing sun; not affected by rain and weather
Sowing: Raising from seed is difficult; usually started from cuttings (see Propagation)
Planting: From mid-May, 8–10 in. (20–25 cm) apart
Care: Keep evenly damp, avoid standing water; feed weekly; deadhead; can be wintered over in a bright place at about 50 °F (10 °C), then cut back shoots by one third in spring
Propagation: From tip cuttings without flower buds; take cuttings from August to March
Design: Well suited for side edges of flowerboxes or as foreground planting in large bowls

Height:
8–24 in.
(20-60 cm)
Bloom Time:
June–
September

herbaceous
perennial

Astilbe Species

Astilbe

Other Name: False spirea
Family: Saxifrage (Saxifragaceae)
Origin: Japan, China, Tibet
Description: Flowers red, pink, white, in candle-like or tuft-like plumes; growth: bushy, erect
Location: Partial shade to shade
Planting: From April; dwarf astilbes in a box, 8–10 in. (20–25 cm) apart; larger ones do best in pots
Care: Always keep well dampened; supply with some delayed-release fertilizer each spring; winter over outdoors with winter protection or indoors in a frost-free spot, light or dark
Propagation: By division or from seed in early spring
Design: Dwarf astilbes can also be combined with other small herbaceous perennials and dwarf woody plants in boxes; taller cultivars are more effective alone.
Species/Cultivars: For planting in pots, dwarf astilbes (*A. chinensis* var. *pumila*) are excellent; if you use other species, you eventually will need large tubs.

Height:
6–12 in.
(15–30 cm)
Bloom Time:
May–
October

herbaceous
perennial
grown as an
annual

Begonia-Semperflorens Group

Wax Begonia

Family: Begonia (Begoniaceae)
Origin: Brazil
Description: Flowers white, pink, red, also bicolored, up to 2 in. (5 cm) across; growth habit: erect, compact; some cultivars have brown-red, dark brown, or bronze-colored foliage
Location: Partial shade to sunny, but preferably not in spots with blazing sun; wind-tolerant
Sowing: Difficult, since seeds must be sown in winter at 72 °F (22 °C) with additional lighting
Planting: From mid-May, 6–10 in. (15–25 cm) apart
Care: Always keep quite moist, but avoid standing water; feed lightly every two to three weeks; regularly remove dead blooms
Design: Pretty in boxes and tall bowls. Good partners are, for example, petunias, verbenas, heliotrope, small fuchsias, sage, and coleus.
Species/Cultivars: *Begonia obliqua* 'Mariebel,' with white flowers, is considered especially free-flowering and robust.

Height:
6–14 in.
(15–35 cm)
Bloom Time:
*May–
October*

*tuberous
plant*

Begonia tuberhybrida Group

Tuberous Begonia

Family: Begonia (Begoniaceae)
Origin: South America
Description: Flowers in shades of yellow, orange, pink, red, and white, usually double; growth habit: erect and spreading or hanging (hanging or pendulous begonias)
Location: Partial shade to shade, some cultivars (especially the small-flowered ones) also in sun; sheltered from wind
Planting: After mid-May, 8–10 in. (20–25 cm) apart; to start, lay tubers close together in boxes with peat or pricking soil in February/March, put in a bright place at 68 °F (20 °C), and keep slightly moist
Care: Keep good and damp, but avoid standing water at all costs; feed lightly every two weeks; remove dead blossoms; wintering over usually not worthwhile for pot cultivation and/or potted cultivars
Propagation: By division of the tubers after new growth appears
Design: Combinations of different-colored cultivars are quite attractive.

Height:
6–8 in.
(15–20 cm)
Bloom Time:
March–June

biennial
summer
flower

Bellis perennis
English Daisy

Other Name: Lawn daisy
Family: Aster, daisy, or sunflower (Asteraceae)
Origin: Europe, Asia Minor
Description: White, pink, or red flowers, some with yellow center; usually double; also resembling pompons or buttons; grows with compact leaf rosette, above which are leafless pedicels
Location: Sunny to partial shade
Sowing: In June/July; light germinator; place in partial shade; prick out into individual pots
Planting: In fall or spring, 4–6 in. (10–15 cm) apart
Care: Water generously on hot days, otherwise keep moderately damp; feed every two weeks; remove dead blooms regularly; if planted in fall, winter over outdoors with some protection or indoors in a bright, cool place, not letting the soil dry out completely
Design: Pretty in combination with blue spring bloomers such as hyacinth and grape hyacinth, also with yellow or white narcissus

Height:
8–20 in.
(20–50 cm)
Bloom Time:
March–May

*herbaceous
perennial,
usually ever-
green*

Bergenia Species

Bergenia

Family: Saxifrage (Saxifragaceae)
Origin: Asia
Description: Bell-shaped flowers in pink, red, or white, in
large false umbels; growth: broad and bushy with usually
evergreen, large, ovate leaves, some turning bronze or reddish
in winter, in some cultivars red throughout the year
Location: Sunny to shade
Planting: From May/June; for seasonal planting, set out in
fall; small specimens 10 in. (25 cm) apart
Care: Keep only slightly moist; in spring, supply with organic
or delayed-release fertilizer; winter over outdoors, with winter
protection in exposed locations
Propagation: By division after the bloom
Design: Very versatile, usable in fall combinations, as spring
bloomers, as decorative foliage plants in summer, for designing shady areas
Species/Cultivars: Low *Bergenia* hybrids as well as *B.
cordifolia* are good for use in planters.

Height:
6–12 in.
(15–30 cm)
Bloom Time:
May–
October

herbaceous
perennial
grown as an
annual

Bidens ferulifolia

Apache Beggarticks

Other Names: Threadleaf tickseed, bur marigold
Family: Aster, daisy, or sunflower (Asteraceae)
Origin: Southern Arizona, Mexico
Description: Golden yellow, star-shaped flowers about 1 in. (3 cm) across; growth: broad, pendulous, with shoots up to 3 ft (1 m) long, and very aggressive/rampant
Location: Sunny, also blazing sun; resistant to wind and weather
Planting: Starting in mid-May, 10–12 in. (25–30 cm) apart
Care: Needs lots of water; ideally, apply delayed-release fertilizer when planting, otherwise feed weekly; winter over at 41–50 °F (5–10 °C) in a bright place, cut back shoots to 6–8 in. (15–20 cm) before bringing indoors
Propagation: From cuttings in August or from wintered over specimens in January–March
Design: Goes well with violet, blue, or red hanging petunias and hanging verbenas, as well as with red or white hanging geraniums; be careful, it can overrun less vigorous plants

Height:
8–12 in.
(20–30 cm)
Bloom Time:
July–
September

annual
summer
flower

Brachyscome iberidifolia
Swan River Daisy

Other Name: Outback daisy
Family: Aster, daisy, or sunflower (Asteraceae)
Origin: Australia
Description: Flowers blue, violet, purple, pink, or white, daisy-like, scented; growth: semipendent, with shoots up to 12 in. (30 cm) long
Location: Sunny, can also be in light shade
Sowing: In March/April; germination temperature of 68–72 °F (20–22 °C)
Planting: Starting in mid-May, 6–8 in. (15–20 cm) apart
Care: Keep evenly and slightly damp; feed lightly every two weeks; if leaves become light in color, add iron supplement; deadhead regularly
Design: Pretty in hanging planters or as underplanting for standards; in boxes, place at front edge or at sides
Species/Cultivars: *B. multifida* has light blue or violet flowers, is a perennial, and can be wintered over; otherwise, it has the same needs as *B. iberidifolia.*

Height:
*8–12 in.
(20–30 cm)*
Bloom Time:
*May–
September*

*semishrub
grown as an
annual*

Calceolaria integrifolia

Slipper Flower

Other Names: Slipper flower, Pocket book flower, pouch flower
Family: Figwort (Scrophulariaceae)
Origin: Chile
Description: Flowers yellow, also flecked with red, panicles
have rounded single flowers; growth habit: bushy, branching;
shoots become pendulous over time
Location: Bright (but not in full sun) or partial shade; protect
from rain
Sowing: Cultivars that can be propagated from seed, in January to February; germination temperature of 59 °F (15 °C)
Planting: Starting in mid-May, 8–10 in. (20–25 cm) apart
Care: Water generously; feed a low dose weekly; deadhead
regularly; can be wintered over in a bright place at 41–50 °F
(5–10 °C)
Propagation: From cuttings, taken in late summer or from
wintered over plants in late January/February
Design: Good in many combinations; does well with partners
such as geraniums (pelargoniums), lobelia, heliotrope, petunias, carnations, begonias, and ageratum

Height:
*6–12 in.
(15–30 cm)*
Bloom Time:
*June–
October*

*annual
summer
flower*

Calendula officinalis

Pot Marigold

Family: Aster, daisy, or sunflower (Asteraceae)
Origin: Mediterranean region
Description: Single or double flowers in yellow, orange, apricot, or cream, often with a dark center, up to 2.5 in. (6 cm) in diameter; erect, compact growth habit
Location: Sunny to partial shade
Sowing: From seed in February/March, germination temperature of 57–61 °F (14–16 °C); alternatively, from April on, sow directly into planter; light germinator
Planting: Starting in early May, 8 in. (20 cm) apart
Care: Keep moderately moist; feed every two weeks; deadhead regularly
Design: Pretty with blue salvia, heliotrope, Cape daisies, salvia, daisies, ageratum; can be easily combined with balcony vegetables and herbs such as tomatoes, arugula, or sage; especially suitable in designs with a country or rustic look
Species/Cultivars: Choose only pot cultivars that stay small, such as 'Little Ball' or the 'Gitana' series

Height:
*8–12 in.
(20–30 cm)*
Bloom Time:
*May–
October*

*herbaceous
perennial
grown as an
annual*

Calibrachoa Hybrids
Trailing Petunias

Other Name: Minipetunias
Family: Nightshade (Solanaceae)
Origin: Presumably Brazil
Description: Flowers red, blue, violet, yellow, orange, apricot, or white, small and funnel-shaped, very numerous; growth: hanging, sprawling, often dense
Location: Sunny, also light shade; newer cultivars generally rain-resistant and not sensitive to wind
Sowing: Not applicable; available for sale only as young plant
Planting: Starting in mid-May, 10–12 in. (25–30 cm) apart; good drainage in planter important
Care: Keep damp but avoid standing water; use soft water for watering, if possible; feed every one to two weeks; no dead-heading needed
Design: For boxes, hanging planters, and hanging baskets; caution: do not plant together with decidedly sensitive or slow-growing partners; pretty, for example, with hanging ver-benas, large-flowered hanging petunias, or Apache beggarticks

Height:
*6–14 in.
(15–35 cm)*
Bloom Time:
*July–
October*

*annual
summer
flower*

Callistephus chinensis

China Aster

Family: Aster, daisy, or sunflower (Asteraceae)
Origin: China
Description: Flowers white, cream, pink, red, violet, blue, often with yellow center, usually fully double, hemispherical to pompon-like, 1.5–4 in. (4–10 cm) in diameter; growth: erect and broad
Location: Sunny
Sowing: In March/April; germination temperature of 59 °F (15 °C)
Care: Water copiously in hot weather, otherwise keep moderately damp and avoid standing water at all costs; feed weekly; deadhead regularly
Design: Attractive in showy mixes with various flower colors even without companions; good partners are daisies, sweet alyssum, lobelia, sage, and—in fall—bushy asters
Species/Cultivars: For use in planters, give preference to so-called dwarf, pot, or bedding asters, which often grow only 8 in. (20 cm) tall

Height:
*8–32 in.
(20–80 cm)*
Bloom Time:
*depending
on cultivar,
June–
December*

*evergreen
dwarf shrub*

Calluna vulgaris
Scotch Heather

Other Name: Ling
Family: Heather (Ericaceae)
Origin: Europe, Asia Minor
Description: Flowers pink, white, red, and violet; growth: erect to prostrate
Location: Sunny to partial shade
Planting: In summer or early fall, 4–8 in. (10–20 cm) apart; for long-term planting, 10–16 in. (25–40 cm) apart; set in rhododendron soil mixed with sand
Care: Keep evenly moist, use soft water; wintering over outdoors possible; in spring cut back by about one third and add rhododendron food
Propagation: From cuttings in August/September
Design: Depending on bloom time, suitable for summer or fall plantings
Tip: The flowers of the so-called bud-blooming cultivars do not open completely, but even the bud shows some color. Thus, they can continue "blooming" well into winter.

Height:
*8–12 in.
(20–30 cm)*
Bloom Time:
*June–
September*

*herbaceous
perennial*

Campanula carpatica

Carpathian Bellflower

Family: Bellflower (Campanulaceae)
Origin: Carpathians (Eastern Europe)
Description: Blue-violet or white bell-shaped flowers that
open like saucers; growth habit: dense, bushy, cushion-like
Location: Sunny to partial shade
Planting: Starting in April, 8–12 in. (20–30 cm) apart
Care: Keep moderately damp; feed a low dose every two
weeks; deadhead; winter over in a frost-free, bright place, if
necessary even outdoors with winter protection
Propagation: By division in spring
Design: The species with compact growth is good in bowls or
boxes; it is also pretty as underplanting for standards
Species/Cultivars: Reliable cultivars are 'Blaue Clips' and
'Weisse Clips,' both only 8 in. (20 cm) high. Others species
are also suitable for use in planters, such as the Serbian
bellflower (*C. poscharskyana*) and the earleaf bellflower
(*C. cochleariifolia*).

Height:
*8–10 in.
(20–25 cm)*
Bloom Time:
*April–
September*

*semishrub
often grown
as an
annual*

Centradenia Hybrids

Centradenia

Other Name: Botanically, also *Heterocentron*
Family: Melastome (Melastomataceae)
Origin: Central America
Description: Small, dainty, intense violet-pink or pink flowers
with a diameter of 3/4 in. (2 cm); overhanging shoots up to
28 in. (70 cm) long; decorative leaves, copper-colored under-
neath
Location: Sunny to partial shade
Sowing: Only from cuttings, not from seed
Planting: After mid-May, 8–10 in. (20–25 cm) apart
Care: Keep evenly and slightly moist; feed a low dose every
two weeks; self-cleaning, do not remove faded blooms; after
hard cutting back in fall may be wintered over in a bright,
cool place
Propagation: From cuttings taken in early spring from wintered over plants
Design: Suitable for hanging planters and mixed boxes and as
underplanting for standards; also very attractive in hanging
baskets

Height:
*8–16 in.
(20–40 cm)*
Bloom Time:
*September–
November*

*herbaceous
perennial
usually
grown as an
annual*

Chrysanthemum x grandiflorum

Chrysanthemum

Other Names: Mum, garden mum; botanically, also *Dendran-
thema* hybrids
Family: Aster, daisy, or sunflower (Asteraceae)
Origin: East Asia
Description: Flowers in all colors except blue, usually double
or pompon-like; growth habit: bushy and branching
Location: Sunny
Sowing: Only from cuttings, not from seed
Planting: For seasonal planting in August/September, 8–12 in.
(20–30 cm) apart
Care: Keep evenly moist; feed once after flowers are fully
open; deadhead; after cutting back can be wintered over in a
bright, cool place, but it is hardly worthwhile since it will not
bloom again until fall
Propagation: Year-round from basal cuttings
Design: Low cultivars for boxes and bowls, tall ones also for
tubs and troughs; good companions are blue bushy asters and
heather

Height:
*6–13 ft.
(2–4 m)*
Bloom Time:
*July–
October*

*climbing
shrub
grown
as an
annual*

Cobaea scandens

Cathedral Bells

Other Name: Cup and saucer vine
Family: Cobaeaceae
Origin: Mexico
Description: Bell-shaped flowers, up to 3 in. (8 cm) long, in violet, red, blue, or white, whitish green when bloom begins; fast-growing twiner with tendrils on its leaves, reddish during the flush
Location: Sunny
Sowing: Starting in late February–March, at a germination temperature of 64–68 °F (18–20 °C); put stake in pot to guide young plants upward
Planting: Starting in mid-May, 20–28 in. (50–70 cm) apart; for single planting use planter of the appropriate size
Care: Large water requirement; feed every two weeks or add timed-release fertilizer when planting; pinch back shoot tips to promote branching; can be wintered over in a bright, cool place, cut back first
Design: From July on, offers rapid-growing and screen; suitable for growing up walls; caution: may crowd other plants

Height:
8–10 in.
(20–25 cm)
Bloom Time:
May–
September

annual
summer
flower

Coleostephus multicaulis

Yellowclump Daisy

Family: Aster, daisy, or sunflower (Asteraceae)
Origin: Algeria
Description: Flowers yellow, in radial arrangement, closed during rain; growth: bushy to cushion-like or slightly trailing; blue-green foliage
Location: Sunny; wind-tolerant
Sowing: In March/April; germination temperature of 59–64 °F (15–18 °C); cover seeds only lightly
Planting: Starting in mid-May, 8 in. (20 cm) apart
Care: Keep evenly and slightly damp; feed every one to two weeks; deadhead regularly
Design: Can be combined with all flowers that do not grow too vigorously; attractive, for example, with red geraniums or carnations, heliotrope, convolvulus; also suitable as under-planting for standards
Species/Cultivars: White-blooming relatives are the mini-marguerite (→ page 75), feverfew (→ page 112), and the marguerite daisy (→ page 129).

Height:
*6–10 in.
(15–25 cm)*
Bloom Time:
*May–
October*

*semishrub
grown
as an
annual*

Convolvulus sabatius

Ground Morning Glory

Family: Bindweed or morning glory (Convolvulaceae)
Origin: Southern Europe, North Africa
Description: Flowers light blue to light violet, funnel-shaped, close up during rain; growth semipendent with shoots up to 3 ft (1 m) long; silvery green foliage
Location: Sunny, also full sun
Sowing: In March; germination temperature of 59 °F (15 °C)
Planting: Starting in mid-May, 8–12 in. (20–30 cm) apart
Care: Keep evenly and slightly damp; feed low doses every two weeks until mid-August; can be wintered over in a bright place at 50 °F (10 °C), shorten shoots first
Propagation: From cuttings from fall to spring
Design: Decorative in hanging planters, also a compatible partner in mixed boxes
Species/Cultivars: Dwarf morning glory (*C. tricolor*), which can be used similarly, has blue, red, pink, or white flowers with a yellow-white throat.

Height:
2–4 in.
(5–10 cm)
Bloom Time:
February–
April

tuberous
plant

Crocus Species

Crocus

Family: Iris (Iridaceae)
Origin: Southern and southeastern Europe, Asia Minor
Description: Cup- or chalice-shaped flowers, yellow, white, pink, purple, or violet, also multicolored; bloom time varies by species and cultivar; growth: erect, short pedicels and grass-like leaves
Location: Sunny, also light shade
Planting: Set out purchased plants in early spring; or bury tubers in the soil at a depth of 2.5–3 in. (6–8 cm) in September/October, 4 in. (10 cm) apart
Care: Water moderately; feed once after bloom begins; winter over fall plantings indoors in a dark, frost-free place or outdoors, covered with pine boughs; don't let soil dry out completely, put in a bright place after new growth appears
Design: Pretty companions for other spring bloomers; also lovely on their own in various flower colors in bowls and boxes, or as a spot of color in permanent plantings

Height:
*6–13 ft
(2–4 m)*
Bloom Time:
*July–
September*

*annual
climber*

Cucurbita pepo

Ornamental Gourds

Family: Gourd (Cucurbitaceae)
Origin: Central America, southern North America
Description: Yellow or white funnel-shaped flowers, 3–4 in. (8–10 cm) long; depending on cultivar, from late summer on, small or large fruit, pear-shaped, egg-shaped, or rounded, green, yellow, white, or striped, inedible; fast-growing climbing plant with large, heart-shaped leaves
Location: Sunny, also light shade; warm; slightly protected, if possible
Sowing: Starting in mid-April, sow two or three seeds in each pot; germination temperature of 64 °F (18 °C); alternatively, sow directly in planters in May
Planting: Starting in mid-May, 24–32 in. (60–80 cm) apart, or singly in large pots
Care: Water copiously in dry weather; feed weekly; provide a stable climbing frame, as the shoots are quite heavy when laden with fruit
Design: Offers attractive, dense screen; the decorative fruits last throughout the winter

Height:
*10–12 in.
(25–30 cm)*
Bloom Time:
*May–
October*

*herbaceous
perennial
grown as an
annual*

Cuphea ignea

Cigar Plant

Other Names: Cigarette plant, firecracker plant
Family: Loosestrife (Lythraceae)
Origin: Mexico
Description: Bright red tubular flowers with black and white lip that is reminiscent of cigar or cigarette ash; growth: heavily branching, with thin, pendulous shoots
Location: Sunny to partial shade, no blazing sun; protect from wind
Sowing: In February/March; germination temperature of 59–64 °F (15–18 °C); pinch back young plants several times
Planting: After mid-May, 8–10 in. (20–25 cm) apart
Care: Keep slightly moist; feed every two to three weeks; can be cut back if necessary
Propagation: From tip cuttings in spring
Design: Pretty with yellow- or white-blooming partners, such as marigolds and dwarf marguerites
Species/Cultivars: *C. ilavea* 'Tiny Mice' has unusual red tubular flowers with blue-violet tips.

Height:
*8–18 in.
(20–45 cm)*
Bloom Time:
*May–
October*

*tuberous
plant*

Dahlia Hybrids

Dahlias

Family: Aster, daisy, or sunflower (Asteraceae)
Origin: Mexico
Description: Flowers white, yellow, pink, bright pink, or red, single, semidouble, or double; growth: bushy and erect
Location: Sunny, also full sun; protected from wind
Sowing: Cultivars that can be grown from seed, in February/March; place two or three seeds in each pot, maintain a germination temperature of 64–68 °F (18–20 °C)
Planting: Starting in mid-May, 12 in. (30 cm) apart, very compact cultivars also slightly closer
Care: Water heavily in hot weather, but avoid standing water; feed weekly; cut off dead flowers regularly; stake tall cultivars; wintering over usually not worthwhile if grown in planters
Design: Small cultivars (such as dwarf mignon dahlias, 'Dahlietta,' 'Dalina') in various flower colors are very effective in balcony boxes; larger ones should be planted singly or in small numbers in pots and tubs.

Height:
*8–12 in.
(20–30 cm)*
Bloom Time:
*June–
September*

*annual
summer
flower*

Dianthus chinensis
Chinese Pink

Other Names: Rainbow pink
Family: Carnation (Caryophyllaceae)
Origin: China, Korea
Description: Flowers pink, red, violet, white, also bicolored, with fringed edges, single or double, up to 3 in. (8 cm) across; growth: broad, bushy
Location: Sun; protected from rain
Sowing: In February/March; germination temperature of 59–68 °F (15–20 °C)
Planting: Starting in mid-May, 8 –10 in. (20–25 cm) apart
Care: Keep evenly and slightly moist; feed every two weeks; cut off dead blooms regularly
Design: Very pretty in color mixes, which can be discreetly accentuated with lobelia, Swan River daisies, or creeping zinnia
Species/Cultivars: For use in planters, the quite similar Sweet William (*D. barbatus*) is an option; the bloom is slightly shorter, but the flowers are fragrant. Another possibility is small carnations (*D. caryophyllus*), some of which are also fragrant.

Height:
*10–12 in.
(25–30 cm)*
Bloom Time:
*May–
October*

*herbaceous
perennial
grown as an
annual*

Diascia-Hybrids

Twinspur

Family: Figwort (Scrophulariaceae)
Origin: South Africa
Description: Small flowers with lipped throats, pink, red, or white; bushy, compact growth, some pendulous shoots
Location: Sunny to partial shade, airy; quite resistant to rain and tolerant of wind
Sowing: January–March; seeds are seldom available for sale, usually available only as young plants
Planting: After mid-May, 8 in. (20 cm) apart
Care: Keep evenly moist; feed every two weeks; can be wintered over in a bright place at 46–50 °F (8–10 °C)
Propagation: From cuttings in spring
Design: Pretty in hanging planters, also suitable for boxes and as underplanting for standards; don't combine with extremely vigorous species
Species/Cultivars: Besides the hybrids, *D. vigilis* (= *D. elegans*) and the annual *D. barbarea* also available; both have pink flowers

Height:
*20–32 in.
(50–80 cm)*
Bloom Time:
April–June

*herbaceous
perennial*

Dicentra spectabilis

Bleeding Heart

Family: Fumitory (Fumariaceae)
Origin: China, Japan, Korea
Description: Heart-shaped pink or white flowers with pro-truding white inner petals that resemble a drop; growth: erect with pendent pedicels; decorative, fern-like foliage, retracts after bloom
Location: Partial shade
Planting: In spring, 10–12 in. (25–30 cm) apart
Care: Keep moderately damp; can be wintered over outdoors with winter protection (pot insulation)
Propagation: From cuttings or by division in spring
Design: These unusual spring and early summer bloomers are very pretty in large bowls or tubs, in combination, for example, with late tulips in pink and white, or with English daisies and forget-me-nots
Tip: The decorative effect is limited to only a few months; consequently, long-term cultivation in a pot is scarcely worthwhile.

Height:
*2–6 in.
(5–15 cm)*
Bloom Time:
*July–
September*

*annual
summer
flower*

Dorotheanthus bellidiformis

Livingstone Daisy

Family: Carpetweed (Aizoaceae)
Origin: South Africa
Description: Flowers in all colors except blue, daisy-like, up to
2 in. (5 cm) across, open only in sunshine; growth: cushion-
forming; fleshy, blue-green leaves
Location: Full sun; protected from rain
Sowing: In March/April, best sown singly in pots; germina-
tion temperature of 61–64 °F (16–18 °C)
Planting: From mid-May on, 4–8 in. (10–20 cm) apart
Care: Keep almost dry; do not feed; deadhead regularly
Design: It usually is sold in color mixtures, so it is pretty even
without companions; good partners are South African daisies
and moss rose
Tip: Closely related and similar in description and care: *Lam-
pranthus* species, which is also available under the name of ice
plant, and *Delosperma pruinosum*, pickle cactus

Height:
*8–12 in.
(20–30 cm)*
Bloom Time:
*September–
December*

*semishrub
grown in
summer*

Erica gracilis
Heather

Other Name: Bell heather
Family: Heather (Ericaceae)
Origin: South Africa
Description: Red, pink, or white bell-shaped flowers, quite abundant in dense racemes; growth: bushy and branching; leaves dark green, needle-shaped
Location: Sunny to partial shade; also tolerates damp, cool weather quite well
Planting: Starting in late August, 8–10 in. (20–25 cm) apart
Care: Keep evenly moist; ideally use soft water for watering
Design: In fall plantings, an attractive partner for dwarf woody plants, bushy asters, and fall mums; also as under-planting for fall-blooming potted woody plants such as *Hebe* x *andersonii* or bluebeard
Species/Cultivars: Unlike the related winter heath (*E. carnea* → page 62), heather is not very frost-hardy and thus is always used as an annual.

61

Height:
6–14 in.
(15–35 cm)
Bloom Time:
December–
April

evergreen
dwarf shrub

Erica herbacea

Winter Heath

Other Names: Herbaceous heath
Family: Heather (Ericaceae)
Origin: Central Europe
Description: Numerous bell-shaped flowers, pink, white, red, or violet; growth: bushy to cushion-like; in some cases, attractive leaf coloration in red-brown, yellow-green, or bronze
Location: Sunny to partial shade
Planting: In fall, 12 in. (30 cm) apart; use acid potting mixture (rhododendron soil) mixed with sand
Care: Keep evenly moist, using soft water if possible; provide rhododendron food in spring, with another one or two doses up to mid-August if needed; possible to winter over outdoors without protection, but insulate planters that contain little soil
Propagation: From softwood cuttings in summer
Design: Pretty in (frost-proof) bowls or boxes, as spot of color in winter between dwarf conifers and other small evergreen woody plants

Height:
*8–12 in.
(20–30 cm)*
Bloom Time:
*May–
September*

*herbaceous
perennial
grown as an
annual*

Erigeron karvinskianus

Mexican Daisy

Other Name: Fleabane
Family: Aster, daisy, or sunflower (Asteraceae)
Origin: South America, southern Europe, northwestern Africa
Description: Numerous small daisy-like flowers, white at first, then pink to red; growth: heavily branching, cushion-like, some pendent shoots
Location: Sun
Sowing: January–March; germination temperature of 59–64 °F (15–18 °C), light germinator
Planting: Starting in mid-May, 8–12 in. (20–30 cm) apart
Care: Keep moderately damp; feed every two weeks; dead-head; can be wintered over in a bright, frost-free place (32–41 °F (0–5 °C)), shorten long shoots beforehand
Design: For hanging planters, mixed boxes, or bowls; can be combined with almost all balcony flowers that are not overly vigorous; adds a Mediterranean flair or a country look
Species/Cultivars: The compact cultivar 'Blütenmeer' has been reliable.

Height:
*10–14 in.
(25–35 cm)*
Bloom Time:
April–June

*semishrub
grown
as a
biennial*

Erysimum cheiri
English Wallflower

Family: Mustard or cabbage (Brassicaceae)
Origin: Southern Europe
Description: Flowers yellow, orange, red, violet, or brown,
~1 in. (2–3 cm) across, in racemes, single or double, with
honey-like scent; growth: erect, bushy, and branching
Location: Sun to partial shade
Sowing: From May–July on; prick out into individual pots
Planting: In fall or spring, 6–8 in. (15–20 cm) apart
Care: Keep evenly and slightly damp; feed every two weeks;
deadhead regularly; for fall planting, winter over outdoors
with protection, and don't let the soil dry out completely
Design: Goes well with all spring bloomers, especially with
blue- and white-flowering partners
Species/Cultivars: For use in planters; the cultivars of the
'Zwergbusch' or 'Bedder' series are a good choice
Tip: Use caution; all parts of the plant, particularly the seeds,
are extremely poisonous!

Height:
10–16 in.
(25–40 cm)
Bloom Time:
June–
October

*annual
summer
flower*

Eschscholzia californica
California Poppy

Other Name: Golden poppy
Family: Poppy (Papaveraceae)
Origin: North America
Description: Flowers yellow, orange, red, pink, or creamy white, goblet-shaped, single or double; open only from late morning to late afternoon and in sun; bushy, branching, cushion-like growth habit
Location: Sunny or full sun
Sowing: In March–April, sow directly into planter; germination temperature of 59 °F (15 °C); thin out later to distance of 10 in. (25 cm)
Planting: Owing to early development of tap root, hard to transplant
Care: Keep slightly damp; no fertilizer; snip off seed capsules
Design: Often sold in color mixes that are highly effective in large boxes, bowls, or tubs
Species/Cultivars: Look for low cultivars, such as 'Dalli' (orange-red) or 'Ballerina' (mixed colors)

Height:
*8–20 in.
(20–50 cm)*
Bloom Time:
*May–
October*

*semishrub
grown
as an
annual*

Felicia amelloides

Blue Marguerite

Other Name: Kingfisher daisy
Family: Aster, daisy, or sunflower (Asteraceae)
Description: Flowers blue with yellow center, resembling daisies; growth: bushy, heavily branching to cushion-like
Location: Sunny, also full sun; tolerates wind
Sowing: February–March, at a germination temperature of 59–64 °F (15–18 °C); pinch back young plants several times
Planting: Starting in mid-May, 10–12 in. (25–30 cm) apart
Care: Keep evenly and slightly damp, but avoid standing water at all costs; feed every two weeks; pinch off withered shoots regularly; winter over in a bright place at 50–54 °F (10–12 °C), especially worthwhile for standards; before moving indoors or the next spring, trim shoots by about one third; keep almost dry during winter
Propagation: From tip cuttings in August/September or in spring; pinch back young plants several times
Design: Pretty in mixed boxes, but can also be decorative alone in pots; lovely as a standard

Height:
*8–16 in.
(20–40 cm)*
Bloom Time:
*May–
October*

*shrub often
grown
as an
annual*

Fuchsia Hybrids
Fuchsia

Family: Evening primrose (Onagraceae)
Origin: South America, Central America, New Zealand
Description: Funnel-shaped flared flowers in red, pink, white, blue-violet, often bicolored; growth: depending on cultivar, bushy and erect, semipendent, or pendent
Location: Prefers half-shade or bright places without direct sun, also thrives and blossoms quite well in shade; protect from wind
Sowing: Sowing from seed is difficult; it is better to buy young plants or to propagate from cuttings
Planting: Starting in mid-May, 8–10 in. (20–25 cm) apart
Care: Keep damp; feed weekly until mid-August; deadhead; for wintering over, see instructions for fuchsias used as container plants (→ page 158), not always worthwhile for small balcony fuchsias
Propagation: From cuttings in spring or late summer
Design: Pendent forms pretty in hanging planters; compact cultivars good for boxes and bowls

Height:
8–10 in.
(20–25 cm)
Bloom Time:
June–
October

herbaceous
perennial
usually
grown as an
annual

Gazania-Hybrids

Gazania

Other Name: Treasure flower
Family: Aster, daisy, or sunflower (Asteraceae)
Origin: South Africa
Description: Flowers yellow, yellow-orange, red, pink, white, often with ring-shaped marking in the center, daisy-like blossoms up to 4 in. (10 cm) across, opening only in sun; shallow leaf rosette, topped by short pedicels
Location: Sunny, preferably full sun; protected from rain
Sowing: February–April; germination temperature of 64–68 °F (18–20 °C)
Planting: Starting in mid-May, 6–8 in. (15–20 cm) apart
Care: Keep only slightly damp; feed weekly; can be wintered over in a bright place at 41–50 °F (5–10 °C)
Propagation: From cuttings taken in late summer, which should be wintered over in a bright, cool place
Design: Very attractive in brilliant color mixes; good partners are blue marguerite, African daisy, heliotrope, or Livingstone daisy; caution: do not combine with plants needing large amounts of water

Height:
*16–24 in.
(40–60 cm)*
Bloom Time:
*July–
October*

*annual
summer
flower*

Helianthus annuus
Sunflower

Family: Aster, daisy, or sunflower (Asteraceae)
Origin: North America, Europe
Description: Flowers yellow, orange, or reddish-brown, with dark center, single or double; growth: erect with sturdy stem; low cultivars also more heavily branching with multiple flowers
Location: Sunny to full sun
Sowing: In April, sow seeds individually in small pots for growing seedlings; germination temperature of 59–68 °F (15–20 °C)
Planting: Starting in mid-May, 8–12 in. (20–30 cm) apart
Care: Needs lots of water; feed weekly; use stakes to support tall cultivars
Design: Cheerful and decorative in summer; dwarf cultivars do well in in large balcony boxes, taller cultivars can be planted individually in containers
Species/Cultivars: Reliable cultivars are 'Sunspot' (single flowers; 16–20 in. (40–50 cm) high), 'Zwerg Sonnengold' (fully double; 16 in. (40 cm)), 'Pacino' (single, branching, 12–16 in. (30–40 cm))

Height:
*12–16 in.
(30–40 cm)*
Bloom Time:
*June–
October*

*herbaceous
perennial
grown as an
annual*

Helichrysum bracteatum

Strawflower

Family: Aster, daisy, or sunflower (Asteraceae)
Origin: Australia
Description: Flowers yellow, orange, pink, red, or white, semi-double or double; growth: bushy to cushion-forming
Location: Sunny to full sun
Sowing: March–April; germination temperature of 64 °F (18 °C); balcony cultivars, however, often cannot be grown from seed
Planting: Starting in mid-May, 8–12 in. (20–30 cm) apart
Care: Keep evenly and slightly damp, but avoid standing water at all costs; feed lightly every two or three weeks; deadheading no longer necessary for modern balcony cultivars, for others, remove faded blooms regularly
Design: Colors bring a hint of country garden, pretty companions: lobelia, hanging verbena, or creeping zinnia
Species/Cultivars: Newer cultivars that can be propagated from cuttings have restored its popularity as a pot plant; 'Golden Beauty', with golden yellow flowers, is also suitable for hanging planters

Height:
12–24 in.
(30–60 cm)
Bloom Time:
May–
September

semishrub
grown
as an
annual

Heliotropium arborescens

Heliotrope

Other Name: Cherry pie
Family: Borage (Boraginaceae)
Origin: Peru
Description: Large umbels in violet or dark blue; intense vanilla scent toward evening; growth: erect, bushy, also available as standard
Location: Sunny; best placed in spot sheltered from wind and rain
Sowing: February–March; germination temperature of 64–68 °F (18–20 °C), light germinator; pinch back young plants
Planting: Starting in mid-May, 10 in. (25 cm) apart
Care: Keep evenly and slightly damp; feed weekly; deadhead regularly; winter over in a bright place at 54–59 °F (12–15 °C), worthwhile only for standards
Propagation: From cuttings in fall or spring
Design: Compact cultivars like 'Mini Marine' go well in boxes with geraniums, marigolds, dwarf marguerites, and sweet alyssum.

Height:
12–24 in.
(30–60 cm)
Bloom Time:
July–August

*herbaceous
perennial*

Hosta Species

Hosta

Family: Hosta (Hostaceae)
Origin: Japan, Korea, China
Description: Flowers white, lilac, or violet, funnel-shaped in clusters on long stalks; growth: broad and in small stands; has large, broad lanceolate to cordate leaves, which depending on species and cultivar are green, bluish, or yellow, often with white or yellow marking
Location: Partial shade to shade
Planting: Starting in March/April; singly in large pots; in nutrient-poor soil (such as special soils for propagating or transplanting), mixed with organic complete fertilizer and expanded clay
Care: Keep moderately damp; add delayed-release fertilizer in spring; winter over outdoors with winter protection or indoors in a frost-free place, light or dark
Propagation: By division in spring or fall
Design: Especially decorative in shady spots; goes well (as neighbor in a separate pot) with fuchsias, astilbe, or ferns

Height:
*6–13 ft.
(2–4 m)*
Bloom Time:
July–August

*herbaceous
perennial
grown as an
annual*

Humulus japonicus

Japanese Hops

Family: Hemp (Cannabaceae)
Origin: Japan, China, Taiwan
Description: Yellowish-green, inconspicuous flowers; fast-growing twiner with vivid green, lobed, large leaves that stay until late in the fall
Location: Sunny to shade
Sowing: February–March; germination temperature of 59–64 °F (15–18 °C); transplant singly into pots, stake young plants immediately
Planting: Starting in mid-May, 16–20 in. (40–50 cm) apart. As it is very invasive, it should only be planted where it can be controlled. This plant is banned in certain areas. Check local regulations.
Care: Needs lots of water, so water heavily, especially in sunny location, but avoid standing water; feed every six to eight weeks
Design: Only a few weeks after planting, it provides a dense visual and wind screen; also hides ugly fences or walls
Species/Cultivars: The cultivar 'Variegatus' has leaves with a whitish-green pattern. It is somewhat less vigorous than the species and tolerates less shade.

73

Height:
*8–12 in.
(20–30 cm)*
Bloom Time:
April–May

*bulbous
plant*

Hyacinthus orientalis

Hyacinth

Family: Hyacinth (Hyacinthaceae)
Origin: Mediterranean region, Near East
Description: Flowers usually blue, violet, pink, white, also yellow or red, dense in cylindrical inflorescences; rosette with stiffly erect, strap-like leaves
Location: Sunny, also light shade; protected from rain
Planting: Set out bud-bearing plants bought in spring, or plant bulbs you have started 6–8 in. (15–20 cm) deep in spring, 6 in. (15 cm) apart
Care: Keep planted bulbs in a frost-free, dark place until they come up, making sure the soil doesn't dry out, then put in a bright place and water moderately; after bloom begins, feed once; protect from late frosts; cut off faded stalks; in pot culture, usually not worth further cultivation
Design: Very pretty in bowls as a mix of cultivars of various colors; lovely companions are herbaceous spring bloomers that cover the bare bottom of the stalk, such as pansies, primrose, English daisies, and forget-me-nots.

Height:
6–12 in.
(15–30 cm)
Bloom Time:
May–
October

annual
summer
flower

Hymenostemma paludosum

Mini-Marguerite

Family: Aster, daisy, or sunflower (Asteraceae)
Origin: Southern Europe, North Africa
Description: Flowers white with golden yellow center, single or double; growth: broad and bushy to pendent
Location: Sunny; wind-tolerant
Sowing: In March/April; germination temperature of 59–64 °F (15–18 °C); cover seeds only lightly with soil
Planting: Starting in mid-May, 8–12 in. (20–30 cm) apart
Care: Keep evenly and slightly damp; feed lightly every one to two weeks; deadhead; cut back after first major array
Design: With the neutral, brightening white of its flowers, the mini-marguerite is well suited to round out and accentuate a wide variety of plant and color combinations; however, don't combine it with extremely vigorous species.
Species/Cultivars: The flowers closely resemble those of the marguerite daisy (→ page 129).

Height:
*8–16 in.
(20–40 cm)*
Bloom Time:
*May–
October*

*herbaceous
perennial
grown as an
annual*

Impatiens 'New Guinea' Group

New Guinea Impatiens

Family: Touch-me-not family (Balsaminaceae)
Origin: Original forms from New Guinea
Description: Flowers red, orange, violet, pink, or white, often in brilliant colors, single or double; growth: broad, also pendent; leaves bronze-colored in some cases or yellow-green with attractive markings
Location: Preferably in partial shade, also in shady or bright spots, but not in blazing sun; protected from rain
Sowing: In February/March; germination temperature of 64–72 °F (18–22 °C)
Planting: After mid-May, 8–12 in. (20–30 cm) apart
Care: Keep quite damp, but avoid standing water; feed low dose every two weeks; deadhead regularly; pinch back frequently to promote branching
Propagation: From cuttings taken in late summer or in spring from wintered over plants
Design: Showy bloomers with intense, brilliant colors for shady places; attractive also owing to decorative leaves in some cases

Height:
*6–12 in.
(15–30 cm)*
Bloom Time:
*May–
October*

*herbaceous
perennial
grown as an
annual*

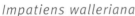

Impatiens walleriana

Impatiens

Other Name: Busy Lizzy
Family: Touch-me-not (Balsaminaceae)
Origin: East Africa
Description: Flowers white, pink, bright pink, red, sometimes bicolored, single or double; growth: heavily branching and quite compact, also pendent
Location: Partial shade, also shade or bright spots, but not in full sun; protected from rain
Sowing: In February/March; germination temperature of 64–72 °F (18–22 °C)
Planting: After mid-May, 6–10 in. (15–25 cm) apart
Care: Keep nicely damp, but avoid standing water at all costs; feed low dose every two weeks; deadhead regularly; pinch back frequently
Propagation: As for New Guinea impatiens (→ page 76)
Design: Often sold in color mixes that are especially pretty in large bowls; in partial shade and shade, pretty partners are fuchsias and begonias, in brighter places also ageratum, hanging verbenas, sweet alyssum, or lobelia

Height:
*6–16 ft
(2–5 m)*
Bloom Time:
*July–
October*

*herbaceous
perennial
grown as an
annual*

Ipomoea lobata

Spanish Flag

Other Names: Firecracker vine; sometimes still known by the botanical name *Quamoclit lobata*
Family: Bindweed (Convolvulaceae)
Origin: Mexico
Description: Flowers tube-shaped, at first scarlet red, then orange, later yellowish white, small, numerous; fast-growing twining plant with three-lobed leaves
Location: Full sun; protected from wind and rain
Sowing: In March–April, sow seeds singly or in small numbers in pots; germination temperature of 64–68 °F (18–20 °C); after about four weeks, prick out into larger pots, provide with small stakes; pinch back young plants
Planting: After mid-May, 12–16 in. (30–40 cm) apart
Care: Keep nicely damp, but do not overwater; feed every one to two weeks; train to grow up climbing frame, pergola, wires, or strings
Design: Quickly creates an attractive visual screen
Tip: The seeds are considered highly poisonous!

Height:
6–10 ft
(2–3 m)
Bloom Time:
*July–
October*

*herbaceous
perennial
grown as an
annual*

Ipomoea purpurea, I. tricolor

Common Morning Glory, Morning Glory

Family: Bindweed (Convolvulaceae)
Origin: Central America and South America
Description: Flowers funnel-shaped, in the common morning glory (→ photo) pink, violet, red, or white with white throat, in the morning glory blue to purple with yellow-white throat; flowers often close by afternoon; twining plants with large heart-shaped or egg-shaped leaves
Location: Full sun; protected from wind and rain
Sowing: As for Spanish flag (→ page 78)
Planting: After mid-May, 12–20 in. (30–50 cm) apart
Care: Keep well dampened but not constantly wet; feed every one to two weeks; train to grow up climbing frame, wires, or strings
Design: The vivid red, purple, or blue shades are a wonderful backdrop for yellow-blooming potted plants or container plants
Tip: The plants themselves are hardly dangerous, but their seeds contain powerful toxins!

Height:
*5–6 ft
(1.5–2 m)*
Bloom Time:
*June–
September*

*annual
climbing
plant*

Lathyrus odoratus

Sweet Pea

Family: Legume (Fabaceae)
Origin: Mediterranean region
Description: Large papilionaceous flowers in loose racemes, pink, red, lilac, white, or apricot, intensely scented; fast-growing climber with pinnatifid leaves
Location: Sunny to partial shade; protected from wind
Sowing: In February/March; sow three or four seeds per pot; germination temperature of 59–64 °F (15–18 °C); starting in mid-April, seed can also be sown directly into planter
Planting: Starting in mid-May, 8–12 in. (20–30 cm) apart
Care: Keep evenly damp; feed weekly; deadhead regularly
Design: Can be combined in large boxes with other plants or used as underplanting
Species/Cultivars: Besides the climbers, there are also bushy, compact cultivars (8–16 in. (20–40 cm) high) for balcony boxes, such as 'Little Sweetheart' and 'Super Snoop,' both available in various shades as color mixes.

Height:
4–8 in.
(10–20 cm)
Bloom Time:
May–
October

*herbaceous
perennial
grown as an
annual*

Lobelia erinus

Lobelia

Other Name: Edging lobelia
Family: Bellflower (Campanulaceae)
Origin: South Africa
Description: Numerous small flowers in many blue shades, violet, pink, some with a white eye, or white: growth: bushy and compact to cushion-forming or hanging, with shoots up to (50 cm) long
Location: Sunny to partial shade
Sowing: January–March at a germination temperature of 64 °F (18 °C); light germinator; prick out into pots in bunches
Planting: Starting in mid-May, 8 in. (20 cm) apart
Care: Keep evenly damp; feed low dose every two weeks; when array declines (usually in July), cut back by one third
Design: As a filler or front planting at the edge of a box or bowl, it rounds out almost every plant combination. Hanging forms are also suitable for overhead planters and as under-planting for standards.

Height:
*3–6 in.
(8–15 cm)*
Bloom Time:
*June–
October*

*annual
summer
flower*

Lobularia maritima

Sweet Alyssum

Family: Mustard or cabbage (Brassicaceae)
Origin: Azores, Canary Islands, Mediterranean region
Description: Flowers white, pink, violet, small, in racemes up to 2 in. (5 cm) long, fragrant; grows flat and cushion-like; slightly pendent; narrow leaves
Location: Sunny to partial shade
Sowing: In March/April; germination temperature of 64 °F (18 °C)
Planting: Starting in mid-May, 6 in. (15 cm) apart
Care: Keep moderately damp; cut back after first array diminishes, then feed once
Design: Undemanding, pretty companion and filler plant for box and bowl edges or as underplanting for standards. The white cultivars in particular can be combined with almost any other balcony flowers or container plants. They accentuate strong flower colors as well as delicate shades. Attractive scented groupings can be created with flowers such as heliotrope, star jasmine, flowering tobacco, or sweet peas.

Height:
*8–16 in.
(20–40 cm)*
Bloom Time:
*June–
September*

*semishrub
grown
as an
annual*

Matthiola incana

Stock

Family: Mustard or cabbage (Brassicaceae)
Origin: Southern Europe, Africa, Asia Minor
Description: Flowers white, yellow, pink, red, or blue, double or single, in loose racemes, intensely scented; growth: erect, bushy, and branching
Location: Sunny, if necessary also partial shade
Sowing: Late March/early April; germination temperature of 59–64 °F (15–18 °C); prick out only the most vigorous seedlings; after thinning out, keep at 50–54 °F (10–12 °C)
Planting: After mid-May, 6–8 in. (15–20 cm) apart; use nonacid potting mix
Care: Keep slightly damp; feed a low dose every two to three weeks
Design: Suitable for use in planters are dwarf stock or low bush stock, usually sold in color mixes; if you place lilies, day lilies, and pot marigolds next to them in separate planters, the balcony will turn into a country garden.

83

Height:
*8–16 in.
(20–40 cm)*
Bloom Time:
*May–
September*

*herbaceous
perennial
grown as an
annual*

Melampodium paludosum

Gold Medallion Flower

Family: Aster, daisy, or sunflower (Asteraceae)
Origin: South America
Description: Rich yellow, orange, or lemon-colored flowers, resembling daisies, ~1 1/2 in. (3–4 cm) across; growth: bushy and branching, compact and cushion-like; vivid green, heart-shaped leaves that accentuate the blossoms' effect
Location: Sunny, also light shade; warm, somewhat protected place
Sowing: In February/March; germination temperature of 68–72 °F (20–22 °C)
Planting: Not until late May (quite sensitive to frost), 10–12 in. (25–30 cm) apart
Care: Keep damp, water generously in hot weather; feed every two weeks; deadhead regularly
Design: Very pretty with other bloomers with strong colors, such as red geraniums, blue-violet petunias, verbenas, or heliotrope; also is attractive in large bowls and tubs, in which the gold medallion flower is combined with such plants as balcony tomatoes

Height:
24–40 in.
(60–100 cm)
Bloom Time:
June–
October

herbaceous
perennial
grown as an
annual

Mirabilis jalapa
Four O'Clock

Family: Bougainvillea (Nyctaginaceae)
Origin: South America
Description: Funnel-shaped flowers in white, yellow, pink, red, violet, also bicolored, even different colors on the same plant; flowers open only in late afternoon and close in early morning, scented; growth: bushy and erect with heart-shaped leaves and often reddish stem
Location: Sunny; warm place
Sowing: March–April; germination temperature of 64–68 °F (18–20 °C)
Planting: Starting in mid-May; singly or 16 in. (40 cm) apart in large pots or roomy planters
Care: Keep evenly damp; feed every two weeks; deadhead regularly
Design: The four o'clock is a special flower, which should be placed wherever you spend the evening, as only then can you fully enjoy the flowers and the delicate fragrance. Smaller hanging plants such as sweet alyssum or lobelia are good as underplanting.

Height:
6–10 in.
(15–25 cm)
Bloom Time:
April–June

*herbaceous
perennial
grown as a
biennial*

Myosotis sylvatica

Forget-Me-Not

Family: Borage (Boraginaceae)
Origin: Europe, Near East
Description: Flowers in many blue shades, pink, or white, numerous tiny individual flowers in dense clusters; growth: bushy and compact
Location: Best in partial shade, but also in sun; preferably cool
Sowing: Sow in July; place in partial shade, prick out singly into pots
Planting: In March or even in fall, 6 in. (15 cm) apart
Care: Water copiously on warm days, but don't keep wet; don't feed; winter over fall plantings outdoors and protect planters from frost, or winter over indoors in a bright, cool place
Design: Very suitable for combining with spring bulbs such as tulips and narcissus, also a pretty partner for English wallflower, pansies, English daisies, or primrose; white and light-blue cultivars in particular make spring arrangements seem lighter and airier

Height:
*4–16 in.
(10–40 cm)*
Bloom Time:
March–May

*bulbous
plant*

Narcissus Species

Narcissus

Family: Amaryllis or daffodil (Amaryllidaceae)
Origin: Mediterranean region
Description: Flowers yellow, orange, or white, trumpet-shaped or star-shaped, in some cases fragrant; growth: erect; strap-like leaves, with one or more pedicels
Location: Sunny to partial shade
Planting: Set out purchased plants in spring or plant bulbs in September, 2–4 in. (5–10 cm) deep; 4 in. (10 cm) apart
Care: Keep slightly damp; after bloom begins, feed once; for fall planting, winter over in a frost-free, dark place, not letting the soil dry out; put bulbs that have been wintered over in a brighter place once growth starts
Design: Plant in small groups; when combining with other species, keep the different bloom times of the narcissus cultivars in mind
Species/Cultivars: Best for use in planters are small wild narcissus, such as *N. bulbocodium,* and low cultivars like *N. pseudonarcissus* (daffodils)

Height:
6–12 in.
(15–30 cm)
Bloom Time:
May–
September

annual
summer
flower

Nemesia Hybrids

Nemesia

Family: Figwort (Scrophulariaceae)
Origin: South Africa
Description: Cup-shaped flowers, white, yellow, orange, pink, red, or blue, up to 1 1/4 in. (3 cm) across, in umbels, in some cases scented; growth: bushy, slightly pendent or hanging
Location: Sunny, also light shade; protected from wind
Sowing: In March/April; germination temperature of 54 °F (12 °C); starting in May, can be sown directly in balcony boxes
Planting: Starting in mid-May, 4–6 in. (15–20 cm) apart
Care: Keep evenly and slightly damp; deadhead; cutting back after the first bloom in June/July will produce a second array; feed once after cutting back
Design: Pretty in color mixes, but also compelling in single colors, especially in bright blue shades; understated companions are lobelia and bacopa
Tip: New cultivated varieties like the 'Karoo' or 'Sunsatia' series eliminate the need for deadheading and cutting back and are also weatherproof.

Height:
12–14 in.
(30–35 cm)
Bloom Time:
July–
September

annual
summer
flower

Nicotiana x sanderae

Tobacco Plant

Family: Nightshade (Solanaceae)
Origin: South America
Description: Flowers in white, cream, yellow, yellow-green, pink, red, violet, tubular with star-shaped crown, in some cases scented; erect, bushy growth habit
Location: Sunny; protected from wind
Sowing: In February/March; germination temperature of 64–68 °F (18–20 °C); light germinator; best to prick out twice
Planting: Starting in mid-May, 10–12 in. (25–30 cm) apart
Care: Needs lots of water; feed weekly; cut off faded flower panicles
Design: Often sold in color mixes that may not need companions; suitable partners are lobelia, creeping zinnia, low marigolds; for flowering tobacco plants with more delicate colors, also petunias and pelargoniums; don't use compact balcony cultivars singly in mixed plantings, but add at least two or three of them as little groups

Height:
6–8 in.
(15–20 cm)
Bloom Time:
June/July–
October

herbaceous
perennial
grown as an
annual

Nierembergia hippomanica

Cupflower

Other Name: Nierembergia
Family: Nightshade (Solanaceae)
Origin: Argentina
Description: Flowers blue, violet, red, or white, with golden yellow center, cup- or goblet-shaped, ~1 in. (2–3 cm) across; growth: broad and cushion-like, later with pendent shoots; delicate, fresh green leaves
Location: Sunny to partial shade; quite weather-resistant
Sowing: In February/March; germination temperature of 64–68 °F (18–20 °C)
Planting: Starting in mid-May, 8 in. (20 cm) apart
Care: Keep well dampened, but avoid standing water; feed weekly; deadhead; winter over in a bright place at about 41–50 °F (5–10 °C)
Propagation: From cuttings taken in August; in a bright place; pinch back young plants
Design: Pretty in boxes and bowls, for example, with yellow-blooming partners; also suitable for hanging planters and as underplanting for standards

Height:
8–16 in.
(20–40 cm)
Bloom Time:
*May–
October*

*herbaceous
perennial
grown as an
annual*

Osteospermum Hybrids

African Daisy

Other Names: South African daisy, Cape daisy, Osteospermum
Family: Aster, daisy, or sunflower (Asteraceae)
Origin: South Africa
Description: Flowers white, yellow, orange, pink, red, lilac, also bicolored, often with dark center, up to 3 in. (8 cm) across, some with spoon-shaped daisy-like flowers, opening only in sunshine; growth: erect, bushy to cushion-forming
Location: Prefers full sun; tolerates wind; does not tolerate steady rain well
Sowing: Not applicable; available only as young plants
Planting: Starting in mid-May, 6–8 in. (15–20 cm) apart
Care: Keep evenly and slightly damp; feed every two weeks; starting in late July, cut off faded parts
Design: Lovely with other sun-loving flowers such as gazania, Livingstone daisies, or blue marguerites
Species/Cultivars: *Dimorphoteca* species are so similar to *Osteospermum* that they also are called African daisies. They are even more sensitive to rain.

91

Height:
*10–14 in.
(25–35 cm)*
Bloom Time:
*May–
October*

*semishrub,
in some
cases
grown as an
annual*

Pelargonium-Peltatum Hybrids

Ivy Geranium

Other Names: Hanging geranium, ivy-leafed pelargonium
Family: Geranium and pelargonium (Geraniaceae)
Origin: South Africa
Description: Flowers red, pink, lilac, white, also bicolored, single or double; growth: semihanging to hanging, with branching shoots up to 5 ft (150 cm) long
Location: Sunny, also partial shade; wind- and weather-resistant, but double-flowering cultivars are more sensitive to rain
Sowing: As for bedding geranium (→ page 93)
Planting: Starting in mid-May, 8–12 in. (20–30 cm) apart
Care: Keep evenly damp; feed weekly; break off faded inflorescences, unless it is a self-cleaning cultivar; winter over in a bright place at 36–41 °F (2–5 °C), keeping almost dry; in February, trim shoots to three or four buds
Propagation: From cuttings taken in August (winter over in bright, cool place) or in February/March
Design: Can be combined with almost all balcony flowers with similar needs, in boxes and hanging planters

Height:
*12–14 in.
(30–35 cm)*
Bloom Time:
*May–
October*

*semishrub,
in some
cases
grown as an
annual*

Pelargonium-Zonale Group

Bedding Geranium

Other Names: Zonal geranium, zonal pelargonium, horseshoe geranium
Family: Geranium and pelargonium
Origin: South Africa
Description: Flowers pink, red, orange, lilac, violet, white, also bicolored, single or double; growth: bushy and erect; leaves often have striking dark ring zone, hence the name zonal geranium/pelargonium
Location: As for ivy geraniums (→ page 92)
Sowing: Sow cultivars that can be reproduced from seed in December/January; germination temperature of 68–75 °F (20–24 °C); prick out twice
Planting: Starting in mid-May, 8–10 in. (20–25 cm) apart
Care: As for ivy geraniums
Propagation: As for ivy geraniums
Design: Versatile in combinations; of all the lovely flower colors, the vivid, brilliant red shades are especially worth mentioning, as these colors otherwise are quite rare in balcony flowers; the "classic" combination: white and bright red geraniums

93

Height:
*1–4 ft
(30–120 cm)*
Bloom Time:
*May–
August*

*semishrub,
in some cases
grown as an
annual*

Pelargonium Species

Scented Geraniums

Other Name: Scented pelargoniums
Family: Geranium and pelargonium (Geraniaceae)
Origin: South Africa
Description: Flowers usually pink, also white or red, small; growth: bushy and erect, spreading, in some cases pendent; leaves scented, emit strong scent when touched
Location: Sunny, *P. odoratissimum* in partial shade
Planting: Starting in mid-May, 12–16 in. (30–40 cm) apart; tall species singly in large pots
Care: Water with restraint, keep only slightly damp; feed every four weeks until mid-August; winter over as for ivy geraniums (→ page 92)
Propagation: As for ivy geraniums (→ page 92)
Design: Depending on growth habit, suitable for boxes, hanging planters, bowls, or tubs
Species/Cultivars: Many species, hybrids, and cultivars with a wide variety of scents, such as *P.* x *graveolens* (rose-scented), *P. odoratissimum* (apple-scented), *P. crispum* 'Minor' (lemon-scented), or *P. fragrans* 'Old Spice' (spicy)

Height:
8–12 in.
(20–30 cm)
Bloom Time:
May–
September

annual
summer
flower

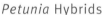

Petunia Hybrids

Common Garden Petunia Hybrids

Family: Nightshade (Solanaceae)

Origin: South America

Description: Flowers in all colors, also multicolored, funnel-shaped or plate-shaped, single or double; growth: bushy and erect to slightly pendent

Location: Sun, bloom is less luxuriant in partial shade; more or less sensitive to rain

Sowing: Starting in January–March; germination temperature of 64–68 °F (18–20 °C); prick out singly into pots

Planting: Starting in mid-May, 8–12 in. (20–30 cm) apart

Care: Needs copious watering; feed weekly, deadhead regularly

Design: Popular partners for geraniums, also pretty with marguerite daisies, marigolds, flowering tobacco plant

Species/Cultivars: Major cultivar groups are 'Grandiflora' (with large flowers, early bloom, quite sensitive to rain), 'Multiflora' and 'Floribunda' (quite rainproof), with medium-sized blossoms, and 'Milliflora' (with small flowers, somewhat sensitive to rain)

Height:
*6–12 in.
(15–30 cm)*
Bloom Time:
*May–
October*

semishrub

Petunia-Hybrids

Hanging Petunias, Small-Flowered

Family: Nightshade (Solanaceae)
Origin: South America
Description: Small to medium-sized funnel-shaped flowers in almost all colors, also multicolored, usually single; growth: semipendent to fully pendent, with shoots up to 32 in. (80 cm) long
Location: Sunny, also partial shade; weatherproof
Sowing: Not reproducible from seed
Planting: Starting in mid-May, 8–12 in. (20–30 cm) apart; ideally in petunia soil
Care: Keep damp but not wet, use soft water; supply with petunia food weekly; no deadheading/cutting back needed
Propagation: From tip cuttings in February/March
Design: Quite attractive in hanging planters and baskets; combine only with vigorous partners
Species/Cultivars: The commercially available cultivar selection is being constantly increased; major cultivar groups include 'Petitunia,' 'Piccolo,' 'Conchita.' Trailing petunias are similar (→ page 44).

P

Height:
*6–12 in.
(15–30 cm)*
Bloom Time:
*May–
October*

*in some
cases
annual,
in others
semishrub*

Petunia-Hybrids

Hanging Petunias, Large-Flowered

Family: Nightshade (Solanaceae)
Origin: South America
Description: Medium-sized to large funnel-shaped flowers in almost all colors, also multicolored, usually single; growth: semipendent or fully pendent, with shoots up to 60 in. (150 cm) long
Location: Sunny, also partial shade; usually rainproof
Sowing: Only F1 hybrids can be grown from seed; proceed as for normal petunia hybrids (→ page 95)
Planting: As for hanging petunias with small flowers
Care: As for hanging petunias with small flowers; wintering over possible for some 'Surfinia' cultivars; to do so, trim shoots to 8 in. (20 cm), keep plants in a bright place at 41–50 °F (5–10 °C)
Propagation: From tip cuttings in February/March
Design: Opulent bloomers for hanging planters and boxes; choose only companions with vigorous growth.
Species/Cultivars: The classics of this group are the 'Surfinia' hybrids, as well as the 'Famous' and 'Cascadias' cultivars, somewhat less vigorous in growth

Height:
*6–12 in.
(15–30 cm)*
Bloom Time:
*July–
September*

*annual
summer
flower*

Phlox drummondii
Annual Phlox

Family: Phlox (Polemoniaceae)
Origin: North America
Description: Single flowers up to 3/4 in. (2 cm) across in white, yellow, pink, violet, in umbel-like inflorescences; broad, bushy growth habit
Location: Sunny
Sowing: March–May; germination temperature of 59 °F (15 °C); pinch back young plants when almost 3 in. (7 cm) high
Planting: Starting in mid-May, 8 in. (20 cm) apart
Care: Keep nicely dampened, but avoid standing water; feed a low dose weekly; deadhead regularly; cutting back after the first main array promotes a second bloom
Design: Often sold in color mixes, it is decorative in boxes or bowls even without partners. Combinations are easily possible, however, and very pretty, for example, with yellow-blooming companions such as slipperwort or Dahlberg daisies.

Height:
*6–12 in.
(15–30 cm)*
Bloom Time:
*August–
September*

*herbaceous
perennial
grown as an
annual*

Plectranthus orsteri

Blue Spur Flower

Other Names: Spurflower, candle plant, Swedish begonia,
prostate coleus; botanically also *P. coleoides*
Family: Mint (Lamiaceae)
Origin: India
Description: White, unprepossessing flowers; very vigorous,
with hanging shoots up to 6 ft (2 m) long; heart-shaped
leaves with aromatic scent, in the commonly used cultivar
'Marginatus' they are edged in white
Location: Sunny to partial shade, if need be in shade
Planting: Starting in mid-May, 8–12 in. (20–30 cm) apart
Care: Keep moderately damp; until mid-August feed every
two weeks; wintering over possible, in a bright place at
50–59 °F (10–15 °C), cut back long shoots beforehand
Propagation: From cuttings in March/April
Design: Plant with ornamental leaves, pretty companion for
summer and fall bloomers that are relatively vigorous, such as
horseshoe geraniums or fall chrysanthemums; can be used in
boxes, hanging planters, or pots

Height:
4–6 in.
(10–15 cm)
Bloom Time:
June–
August

annual
summer
flower

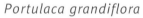

Portulaca grandiflora

Moss Rose

Family: Purslane (Portulacaceae)
Origin: South America
Description: Flowers yellow, orange, red, bright pink, pale pink, or white, bowl-shaped, up to 3 in. (8 cm) across, single or double, open only in sunshine; growth: prostrate to trailing, flat shoots
Location: Best in full sun; protected from rain
Sowing: March–May; germination temperature of 64 °F (18 °C); after early May can be directly sown in balcony box
Planting: Starting in mid-May, 6 in. (15 cm) apart
Care: Water with restraint, avoid standing water at all costs; feed every four to six weeks
Design: The gay color mixes, despite their low growth habit, can embellish boxes, bowls, or even hanging planters. Potential partners must also do well in full sun with very little water; suitable ones are, for example, African daisies, Livingstone daisies, or gazania.

Height:
*2–6 in.
(5–15 cm)*
Bloom Time:
*February–
May*

*herbaceous
perennial
grown as an
annual*

Primula vulgaris ssp. *Vulgaris*

Primrose

Family: Primrose (Primulaceae)
Origin: Europe, Asia Minor, North Africa
Description: Flowers in all colors except pure blue, but including violet, also multicolored, contrasting yellow or orange center, plate-shaped, 3/4–2 in. (2–5 cm) across, in umbels; slightly scented; cushion-shaped leaf rosette
Location: Sunny to partial shade
Sowing: Difficult; better to buy plants, starting in February
Planting: In spring, 6–8 in. (15–20 cm) apart
Care: Keep evenly and slightly damp, do not overwater; no feeding necessary
Design: Bowls with cultivars of different colors provide a cheerful, spring-like atmosphere; suitable partners are spring bulbs like narcissus, pansies, and forget-me-nots.
Tip: If you have a garden, you can plant the cushion-forming primroses there after the bloom and keep cultivating them for many years.

Height:
*8–16 in.
(20–40 cm)*
Bloom Time:
March–June

*tuberous
plant*

Ranunculus asiaticus

Persian Buttercup

Family: Buttercup (Ranunculaceae)
Origin: Mediterranean region, Africa
Description: White, yellow, orange, pink, or red, fully double flowers 2–4.5 in. (5–12 cm) across; growth: erect, with several pedicels
Location: Sun to partial shade
Planting: Set out purchased plants from April on, or plant the claw-like tubers in spring or fall, at most 2 in. (5 cm) deep ("claw tips" pointing downward); 8 in. (20 cm) apart
Care: Keep evenly damp; feed low dose every one to two weeks; for fall planting, winter over in a frost-free, dark place, not letting soil dry out completely; once growth begins, put in a bright to partially shaded place
Propagation: By tuber division in fall, some cultivars also from seed in spring
Design: Especially attractive with mixed flower colors in large bowls; pretty with blue companions like forget-me-nots or blue tufted pansies

Height:
*12–32 in.
(30–80 cm)*
Bloom Time:
*May–
October*

*herbaceous
perennial
grown as an
annual*

Salvia farinacea

Blue Sage

Other Names: Mealycup sage, mealy sage
Family: Mint (Lamiaceae)
Origin: North America, Mexico
Description: Small labiate flowers in densely filled whorls arranged like ears of corn, blue, violet, or white; growth: stiffly erect, densely branching; with lanceolate, overhanging leaves, in some cases whitish gray and felt-like
Location: Sunny, also full sun
Sowing: February–April; germination temperature of 64–68 °F (18–20 °C)
Planting: After mid-May, depending on height when grown, 8–14 in. (20–35 cm) apart
Care: Keep evenly damp but not wet; feed low dose weekly
Design: Makes a nice backdrop behind larger boxes or bowls; yellow, red, or white flowers of other summer bloomers are very effective in front; good partners are pot marigolds and marigolds, marguerites, or geraniums.

Height:
*8–12 in.
(20–30 cm)*
Bloom Time:
*May–
September*

*herbaceous
perennial
grown as an
annual*

Salvia splendens
Scarlet Sage

Family: Mint (Lamiaceae)
Origin: Brazil
Description: Labiate flowers in long racemes, bright red, violet, or salmon pink; growth: erect, bushy
Location: Sunny; if possible, protected from rain and wind
Sowing: In February/March; germination temperature of 68–72 °F (20–22 °C); pinch back when 3 in. (8 cm) high; the tips can be planted as cuttings
Planting: Starting in mid-May, 8–12 in. (20–30 cm) apart
Care: Keep evenly damp; feed low dose weekly; cut off faded, brown inflorescences
Design: Brightly colored partner for yellow, blue, or white flowers like marigolds and lady's slippers, heliotrope or dwarf marguerites
Species/Cultivars: Dependable compact cultivars are, for example, 'Johannisfeuer' (scarlet red) and 'Laser Purple' (dark violet); both 10 in. (25 cm) high

Height:
*3–6 in.
(8–15 cm)*
Bloom Time:
*June–
October*

*annual
summer
flower*

Sanvitalia procumbens

Creeping Zinnia

Other Name: Spreading yellow zinnia
Family: Aster, daisy, or sunflower (Asteraceae)
Origin: Mexico, Guatemala
Description: Yellow, star-shaped flowers with brown-black center, ~1 in. (2–3 cm) across; branching, prostrate to pendent shoots
Location: Sunny; protected from rain
Sowing: In March; germination temperature of 64 °F (18 °C)
Planting: Starting in mid-May, 4–6 in. (10–15 cm) apart
Care: Keep slightly damp at all times; feed low dose every two weeks; cut off withered shoots
Design: Pretty in front along the edge of a box, also good in hanging planters or as underplanting for tub plants
Species/Cultivars: An additional species is *S. speciosa*, commonly known as Sunbini sanvitalia. It has golden yellow flowers and shoots up to 32 in. (80 cm) long, is very suitable for use in hanging planters, and can be combined even with vigorous hanging petunias.

Height:
8–12 in.
(20–30 cm)
Bloom Time:
May–October

herbaceous perennial usually grown as an annual

Scaevola saligna

Fan Flower

Family: Goodenia (Goodeniaceae)
Origin: Pacific islands, Australia
Description: Violet or blue flowers, shaped like little fans; growth: bushy, spreading, and semipendent, with shoots up to 3 ft (1 m) long
Location: Sunny to partial shade; rainproof
Sowing: Not applicable; can be propagated only from cuttings
Planting: Starting in mid-May, 8–12 in. (20–30 cm) apart
Care: Keep damp; tolerates dryness temporarily, but not standing water; feed low dose weekly; self-cleaning; winter over in bright place at 50–59 °F (10–15 °C); cut back in spring
Propagation: From tip cuttings taken in fall or spring
Design: With its overflowing, upward-arching branches, it can fill a hanging planter on its own, but it can also be combined with other plants in boxes, wide pots, or hanging baskets.

Height:
*12–20 in.
(30–50 cm)*
Bloom Time:
*September–
October*

*herbaceous
perennial*

Sedum Species

Stonecrop

Family: Orpine (Crassulaceae)
Origin: Europe, Siberia, Asia
Description: Flowers pink, crimson, or purplish red, in large umbels; growth: erect, with fleshy leaves
Location: Sunny
Planting: Set out container-grown plants in summer; plant singly in pots, or 12–16 in. (30–40 cm) apart
Care: Keep moderately damp; add slow-release fertilizer when planting; after wintering over, feed every four weeks from spring to August; cut back withered shoots in spring; winter over outdoors with winter protection, or indoors in a bright, cool place, keeping it almost dry
Propagation: From cuttings taken in spring or early summer
Design: Can be combined in tubs with low fall bloomers and foliage plants
Species/Cultivars: Attractive stonecrops for pots are
S. telephium 'Herbstfreude' and *S. spectabile*

Height:
*8–12 in.
(20–30 cm)*
Bloom Time:
none

*semishrub
grown
as an
annual*

Senecio cineraria

Dusty Miller

Family: Aster, daisy, or sunflower (Asteraceae)
Origin: Southern Europe
Description: The yellow flowers appear only in long-term cul-ture, starting the second summer; growth: bushy and branch-ing; whitish or greenish silvery leaves, lobate or laciniate; numerous forms and/or cultivars
Location: Sunny; protected from rain
Sowing: Starting in January–March; germination temperature of 64 °F (18 °C)
Planting: Starting in mid-May or in late summer, 8–12 in. (20–30 cm) apart
Care: Keep only slightly damp; feed low dose every two weeks
Design: Ornamental foliage plant; in colorful plantings, use dusty miller to create a good balance and a resting point for the eye. The silvery leaf color lends an elegant note to restrained combinations with blue, violet, white, and pink tones.

Height:
*8–16 in.
(20–40 cm)*
Bloom Time:
*July–
September*

*herbaceous
perennial
grown as an
annual*

Solenostemon scutellarioides

Coleus

Other Names: Painted nettle; formerly known as *Coleus blumei* hybrids
Family: Mint (Lamiaceae)
Origin: Southeast Asia, Africa
Description: Flowers blue-white, inconspicuous; growth: bushy; egg-shaped to heart-shaped leaves, serrate or undate on the edges, usually multicolored, depending on cultivar, in various shades of green, red, pink, and yellow, also almost black, with various patterns
Location: Sunny to partial shade; has the best coloring in partial shade
Sowing: January–February; germination temperature of 68–75 °F (20–24 °C)
Planting: Starting in mid-May; 8–10 in. (20–25 cm) apart
Care: Keep moderately damp; feed every two weeks; if flower panicles appear, break them off immediately
Propagation: From cuttings in fall or spring
Design: As an ornamental foliage plant, painted nettle is a very pretty partner for blue, yellow, or white bloomers.

Height:
*8–10 in.
(20–25 cm)*
Bloom Time:
*April/May–
October*

*semishrub
grown
as an
annual*

Sutera diffusus
Bacopa

Family: Figwort (Scrophulariaceae)
Origin: South America
Description: Flowers in white or pale pink, small, star-shaped, very numerous; growth: creeping to trailing, shoots up to 40 in. (100 cm) long
Location: Sunny to partial shade; tolerates wind
Sowing: Not applicable, available only as young plant
Planting: Starting in mid-May, 8–10 in. (20–25 cm) apart
Care: Keep evenly damp; feed every two weeks; self-cleaning, no deadheading necessary
Design: With its luxuriant growth and wealth of blooms, bacopa will fill hanging planters even unaccompanied, but it also can be combined in hanging arrangements and in boxes with all balcony flowers that are not overly vigorous
Tip: Cultivars with somewhat larger flowers are especially apt to stop blooming for short periods on occasion.

Height:
*6–12 in.
(15–30 cm)*
Bloom Time:
*May–
October*

*annual
summer
flower*

Tagetes Species and Hybrids

Marigold

Family: Aster, daisy, or sunflower (Asteraceae)
Origin: Mexico
Description: Flowers yellow, orange, red, reddish brown, also multicolored, in *T. tenuifolia* single, in *T. patula* hybrids usually double; growth: erect, bushy
Location: Sunny, also light shade; wind- and rainproof (*T. tenuifolia* is especially robust)
Sowing: Starting in January–March; germination temperature around 64 °F (18 °C); starting in mid-April can also be sown directly into planter
Planting: Starting in mid-May, 6–10 in. (15–25 cm) apart
Care: Keep moderately damp; feed weekly; deadhead regularly
Design: Marigolds enrich mixed plantings with their warm, brilliant colors
Tip: Marigolds have a lemony to sharp scent, sometimes also penetrating. The *T. tenuifolia* cultivars, however, are more aromatic in scent.

Height:
*10–24 in.
(25–60 cm)*
Bloom Time:
*June–
September*

*herbaceous
perennial
grown as an
annual*

Tanacetum parthenium
Feverfew

Other Names: Featherfew, featherfoil
Family: Aster, daisy, or sunflower (Asteraceae)
Origin: Europe
Description: Flowers white with yellow center or yellow, single or double, in some cases scented; growth: erect, broad, bushy
Location: Best placed in sun, bloom is weaker in partial shade
Sowing: In March/April; germination temperature of 59–64 °F (15–18 °C); cover seed only thinly with soil
Planting: Starting in mid-May, 8–12 in. (20–30 cm) apart
Care: Keep evenly damp; feed every two weeks; deadhead regularly
Design: Low cultivars up to 12 in. (30 cm) high are useful in mixed balcony boxes or bowls; high cultivars are more rarely used in planters, but look pretty in large pots or tubs
Species/Cultivars: Closely related: the mini-marguerite (→ page 75) and yellowclump daisy (→ page 51)

Height:
3–6 ft
(1–2 m)
Bloom Time:
*June–
October*

*herbaceous
perennial
grown as an
annual*

Thunbergia alata

Black-Eyed Susan Vine

Family: Acanthus (Acanthaceae)
Origin: East Africa
Description: Flowers yellow, orange, or white, usually with black eye, shaped like a shallow funnel, 3/4–2 in. (2–5 cm) across; twining plant, moderately vigorous growth, hanging without support; heart-shaped, bright green leaves
Location: Sunny, even full sun; if possible, protected from wind and rain
Sowing: February–March, three or four seeds per pot; germination temperature of 64 °F (18 °C); pinch back young plants
Planting: Starting in mid-May, 8–16 in. (20–40 cm) apart
Care: Keep evenly damp, avoid standing water; feed every two weeks; prune some shoots occasionally to promote better branching; wintering over not always worthwhile, but possible, in a bright place at 41–50 °F (5–10 °C); then cut back vigorously in spring
Design: Also attractive as hanging plant in planters and large mixed boxes

Height:
6–8 in.
(15–20 cm)
Bloom Time:
June–
October

annual
summer
flower

Thymophylla tenuiloba

Dahlberg Daisy

Other Names: Botanically, also *Dyssodia tenuiloba*
Family: Aster, daisy, or sunflower (Asteraceae)
Origin: Mexico
Description: Daisy-like, yellow star flowers, ~3/4 in. (1–2 cm) across; growth: broad, with overhanging shoots
Location: Sunny, also full sun
Sowing: Starting in February–March; germination temperature of 64–68 °F (18–20 °C)
Planting: Starting in mid-May, 6–8 in. (15–20 cm) apart
Care: Always keep slightly damp, but avoid standing water; feed low dose every two weeks; deadhead regularly
Design: Especially attractive in hanging planters, also as hanging accompaniment at the edge of a box or as underplanting for standards, as under Paraguay nightshade, Cape plumbago, pomegranate, or rose standards; very pretty are combinations with Swan River daisies (*Brachyscome* → page 41); don't plant with very vigorous plants like hanging petunias or Apache beggarticks

Height:
*10–12 in to
10 ft (25–30
cm to 3 m)*
Bloom Time:
*July–
October*

*herbaceous
perennial
grown as an
annual*

Tropaeolum majus

Nasturtium

Family: Nasturtium (Tropaeolaceae)
Origin: South America
Description: Flowers yellow, creamy white, orange, red; single, semidouble, or double, up to 2 in. (5 cm) across; growth: bushy or creeping to hanging, climbing cultivars up to 10 ft (3 m) high; shield-shaped (peltate) leaves
Location: Prefers sun, also partial shade
Sowing: In March/April; germination temperature of about 64 °F (18 °C); can also be sown directly into planter in May
Planting: Starting in mid-May; compact cultivars 10 in. (25 cm) apart, others at least 12 in. (30 cm) apart
Care: Keep moderately damp; feed every two weeks, using low-nitrogen food if possible; if leaves proliferate, omit feeding for several weeks
Design: Bushy cultivars are pretty in pots or boxes; use long-stemmed cultivars in hanging planters or as climbers
Tip: Closely related: the climbing Canary creeper (→ page 116).

Height:
*3–10 ft.
(1–3 m)*
Bloom Time:
*July–
October*

*annual
climbing
plant*

Tropaeolum peregrinum
Canary Creeper

Other Name: Canary bird flower
Family: Nasturtium (Tropaeolaceae)
Origin: South America
Description: Numerous lemon yellow flowers with heavily fringed petals, about 1 in. (3 cm) across; fast-growing climber with large, hand-shaped lobate leaves, slightly bluish green in color
Location: Sunny to partial shade; somewhat protected
Sowing: In March, sow two or three seeds in each pot; germination temperature of about 61 °F (16 °C); add stakes when pricking out
Planting: Starting in mid-May, 16–24 in. (40–60 cm) apart
Care: Keep moderately damp; feed every two weeks, using low-nitrogen food if possible
Design: Canary creeper, a close relative of the nasturtium (→ page 115), will swiftly climb up latticework, fences, and walls, and its unusual fringed flowers are quite attractive. For a pretty underplanting, use blue- or red-blooming flowers.

Height:
*4–16 in.
(10–40 cm)*
Bloom Time:
March–May

*bulbous
plant*

Tulipa Species and Hybrids

Wild Tulip, Botanical Tulip

Family: Lily (Liliaceae)
Origin: Asia
Description: Flowers in all colors except blue, also multicolored; cup-, bell-, or star-shaped, in some cases scented, bloom time varies by species and cultivar; growth: erect, single stem, with lanceolate, pointed leaves
Location: Sunny to partial shade
Planting: As for garden tulips (→ page 118)
Care: As for garden tulips (→ page 118); for small wild tulips, however, dispense with feeding altogether
Design: For optimum effect, always plant in small groups of four or five
Species/Cultivars: Very pretty are low wild tulips such as *T. clusiana* (flower white with pink, 6–12 in. (15–30 cm) high). Also suitable: botanical tulips (hybrids of wild species); these include the Kaufmanniana, Fosteriana, and Greigii tulips, which are available in numerous flower colors, often also multicolored with striking markings.

117

Height:
*8–16 in.
(20–40 cm)*
Bloom Time:
March–May

*bulbous
plant*

Tulipa Hybrids

Garden Tulip

Family: Lily (Liliaceae)
Origin: Asia
Description: Flowers in all colors except blue, also multicolored; usually goblet-shaped, single or double, in some cases scented, bloom time varies by cultivar; growth: erect, single stem, with lanceolate, pointed leaves
Location: Sunny to partial shade
Planting: Set out purchased plants in spring, or plant bulbs 4 in. (10 cm) deep in September; 4 in. (10 cm) apart
Care: Keep moderately damp; feed once after bloom begins; cut off withered stalks at halfway point; for fall planting, winter over in a frost-free, dark place, move to bright spot or partial shade once new growth begins
Design: Suitable partners are, for example, narcissus, forget-me-nots, or horned violets
Species/Cultivars: Best suited for planters are low cultivars of the so-called single early tulips. Wild tulips (→ page 117) are also quite charming.

Height:
*8–16 in.
(20–40 cm)*
Bloom Time:
*June–
October*

*herbaceous
perennial
grown as an
annual*

Verbena Hybrids
Garden Verbena

Other Name: Vervain
Family: Verbena (Verbenaceae)
Origin: South America
Description: Flowers in blue, violet, white, red, or pink, umbel-like inflorescences with tiny individual blooms; growth: erect, bushy; broad-leaved or fine-leaved
Location: Sunny; modern cultivars are weatherproof
Sowing: Difficult, better to buy young plants
Planting: Starting in mid-May, 8–12 in. (20–30 cm) apart
Care: Keep well dampened, but don't soak substrate; feed every two weeks; deadhead regularly
Design: Attractive in boxes, for example, with geraniums, marigolds, African daisies, or dusty miller
Species/Cultivars: The reliable erect verbenas like 'Derby' or 'Novalis' have to some extent faded into the background owing to the great popularity of the hanging verbenas (→ page 120), but they are worth planting, as are newer compact cultivars such as the 'Babylon' cultivar group.

119

Height:
*8–10 in.
(20–25 cm)*
Bloom Time:
*June–
October*

*herbaceous
perennial
grown as an
annual*

Verbena Hybrids

Hanging Verbena

Other Names: Vervain, herb of grace
Family: Verbena (Verbenaceae)
Origin: South America
Description: Flowers blue, violet, red, pink, or white in
umbel-like inflorescences, densely packed with individual
flowers; growth habit: hanging; fine- or broad-leaved
Location: Sunny; weather-resistant
Sowing: Usually not reproducible from seed
Planting: Starting in mid-May, 8–12 in. (20–30 cm) apart
Care: Needs abundant watering, but sensitive to standing
water; feed weekly; deadhead
Design: Good partners for the vigorous hanging verbenas are
highly competitive species such as hanging geraniums, trailing
petunias, or Apache beggarticks.
Species/Cultivars: Frequently available are Temari and Tapien
verbenas, as well as similar newer cultivars (such as the
'Tukana' series). They are usually vigorous, bear many blossoms, have strong colors, and are quite rain-tolerant.

Height:
*4–6 in.
(10–15 cm)*
Bloom Time:
April–June

*(fall)
usually
biennial*

Viola-Cornuta Hybrids

Horned Violet

Other Name: Tufted pansy
Family: Violet (Violaceae)
Origin: Pyrenees, Spain
Description: Flowers in all colors, usually multicolored, small, very numerous; growth: compact, in some cases trailing
Location: Sunny to partial shade
Sowing: For spring blooming, in July–August; start in partial shade, after pricking out, put in a brighter place
Planting: In March/April, 4–8 in (10–20 cm) apart
Care: Water generously on warm days; feed once at most; cut off withered pedicels; winter over your cultivated plants in a bright, cool place (at 36–41 °F (2–5 °C))
Design: Lovely companions for late-blooming tulips and narcissus, as well as English wallflower
Tip: Depending on cultivar and sowing time, horned violets—like pansies (→ page 122)—bloom in spring, in summer, or not until fall. They are more important, however, for their decorative value in spring.

Height:
*6–10 in.
(15–25 cm)*
Bloom Time:
March–June

*(fall)
biennial
summer
flower*

Viola x wittrockiana

Pansy

Family: Violet (Violaceae)
Origin: Europe
Description: Flowers in all colors, also multicolored, small or large; growth: compact, bushy
Location: Sunny to partial shade
Sowing: In June/July; start in partial shade; prick out into individual pots, then put in a brighter place
Planting: In fall or spring, 4–6 in. (10–15 cm) apart
Care: Keep evenly damp; feed every two to three weeks; dead-head regularly; your own cultivated plants can be wintered over outdoors with good winter protection, or indoors in a bright, cool spot
Design: Often available are color mixes, which help create wonderfully colorful spring bowls and boxes. Pansies go well with tulips, narcissus, hyacinth, or grape hyacinth, but they can also beautify fall plantings; for this purpose, it is best to buy already blooming plants late in the year.

Height:
6–12 in.
(15–30 cm)
Bloom Time:
July–
September

annual
summer
flower

Zinnia angustifolia, Z. elegans

Zinnia

Family: Aster, daisy, or sunflower (Asteraceae)
Origin: Mexico, Central America
Description: Flowers yellow, orange, white, pink, red, or violet, also bicolored, single or double, up to 4 in. (10 cm) across; growth: erect, bushy
Location: Sunny; protected from wind and rain, if possible
Sowing: From February to May; germination temperature of about 68 °F (20 °C)
Planting: Not until late May, as it is somewhat sensitive to frost; 6–8 in. (15–20 cm) apart
Care: Keep evenly damp; feed every two weeks; deadhead regularly
Design: Zinnias can be combined with a number of other balcony flowers; the warm, sometimes very brilliant hues create a lively effect.
Tip: Some *Z. elegans* cultivars, with their fully double flowers, resemble low dahlias; small-flowered, single *Z. angustifolia* cultivars, on the other hand, have almost a rustic look.

Container Plants
from A to Z

Mediterranean flair, tropical splendor, enchanting exotic blooms—growing plants in containers and tubs will make these settings possible for you to achieve, since the props can be brought to a protected place for the winter. But the more robust potted woody plants, too, have much to offer, and they often provide attractive decoration during the cold months of the year when competitors are absent from the scene.

Height:
3–10 ft
(1–3 m)
Bloom Time:
April–
October

shrub, in
some cases
evergreen

A

Abutilon Hybrids and Species

Flowering Maple

Other Name: Chinese bellflower
Family: Mallow (Malvaceae)
Origin: Brazil
Description: Flowers yellow, orange, red, pink, or white, large calyxes, blooms year-round in bright location; growth: erect, widely branched; large, lobed leaves, in some cultivars spotted with yellow or white
Location: Sunny, but not blazing sun; warm, if at all possible; protected from wind and rain
Care: In summer, keep well dampened but not wet; until August, feed every one to two weeks; deadhead; winter over in a bright place at 41–50 °F (5–10 °C)
Propagation: From tip cuttings or from seed in spring; pinch out young plants several times
Design: Very attractive also as standard
Species/Cultivars: In addition to the *Abutilon* hybrids, *A. megapotamicum*, with overhanging shoots, and the more delicate *A. pictum* are also pretty in containers or tubs.

Height:
*up to 3 ft
(1 m)*
Bloom Time:
*January–
February*

*evergreen
succulent*

Aeonium arboreum

Aeonium

Family: Orpine (Crassulaceae)
Origin: Southern Europe, Morocco
Description: Flowers yellow, in container culture, however, rare and appearing only on older specimens; growth: tree-like, branching, with thick, fleshy leaf rosettes, which in the cultivar 'Atropurpureum' are brownish red to blackish red in color
Location: Sunny, also full sun; protected from rain
Care: Water only when topmost soil layer is dried out; avoid standing water at all costs; until August, supply with cactus food every two weeks; winter over in a bright place at 50–54 °F (10–12 °C), if need be can also be kept warmer, almost dry in a bright place
Propagation: From tip cuttings (entire rosettes with piece of stem)
Design: Looks lovely in terra-cotta pots; the blackish-red 'Atropurpureum' is especially attractive in blue- or white-glazed containers; however, it can also be arranged very hand-somely with colorful summer flowers as neighbors

Height:
*2.5–4 ft
(0.8–1.2 m)*
Bloom Time:
July–August

*herbaceous
perennial,
in some
cases ever-
green*

A

Agapanthus Hybrids, *A. praecox*

African Lily

Family: Onion, garlic, or leek (Alliaceae)
Origin: South Africa
Description: Flowers in blue, violet, or white, funnel-shaped, very numerous in umbels; grows in broad clumps of strap-shaped leaves, above which the erect pedicels rise
Location: Sunny
Care: Water copiously on hot days, but avoid standing water; feed every one to two weeks until August; repot rarely, into only slightly bigger containers, otherwise flowering will be reduced at first; winter over in a moderately bright place at 39–46 °F (4–8 °C), keeping evergreen forms slightly damp and deciduous forms dry
Propagation: By division in spring or after the bloom
Design: Especially good combined with yellow-blooming container plants or summer flowers
Tip: If the bloom is poor, the cause is apt to be overly warm temperatures during wintering over or nitrogen-rich feeding

Height:
*20–60 in.
(0.5–1.5 m)*
Bloom Time:
*not
applicable*

*evergreen
succulent*

Agave americana

Century Plant

Family: Agave (Agavaceae)
Origin: Mexico, Mediterranean region
Description: Yellow flowers, very rare in container culture, plant dies back after bloom; broad rosette of long, lanceolate leaves, bluish green, yellow- or white-edged or striped, with sharp spines on the tips and margins
Location: Sunny, also full sun or partial shade; protect from rain
Care: Keep moderately damp, better drier than too wet; in spring supply with cactus food; winter over in a bright place at 41 °F (5 °C), keep almost dry
Propagation: From suckers, which should be carefully removed and newly planted
Design: Ornamental leaves are striking next to other Mediterranean or South American plants
Tip: Be careful, the sharp spines can cause injury! Before transporting, stick corks on the dangerous spines.

Height:
*20–60 in.
(0.5–1.5 m)*
Bloom Time:
*May–
October*

*evergreen
semishrub*

A

Argyranthemum frutescens
Marguerite Daisy

Family: Aster, daisy, or sunflower (Asteraceae)
Origin: Canary Islands
Description: Flowers white, pink, or yellow, depending on cultivar single or double, blooms year-round in bright location; broad, bushy growth; leaves pinnate, usually blue-green
Location: Sunny, also full sun
Care: Water copiously in hot weather; feed weekly until August; cut off withered parts regularly, or shorten all shoots by one third after the first primary bloom; remove brown leaves; winter over in as bright a place as possible at 39–46 °F (4–8 °C), keeping slightly damp and cutting back in spring; if need be, winter over in a dark place, but then cut back by half first and keep almost dry
Propagation: From cuttings in spring; pinch back young plants several times
Design: Lovely long-term bloomer that doesn't need lots of space; pretty as a standard; compact cultivars are also suitable in mixed balcony boxes

Height:
*20–30 in.
(0.5–1.5 m)*
Bloom Time:
*March–
April*

*evergreen
shrub*

Aucuba japonica

Japanese Aucuba

Family: Dogwood (Cornaceae)
Origin: Japan, China, Taiwan
Description: Flowers reddish, inconspicuous; growth: broad, bushy; large, pointed, shiny ovate leaves, in some cultivars spotted or dotted with yellow; bright red, toxic (!) berries only on female plants
Location: Partial shade to shade; protected from rain and to some extent from wind
Care: Keep evenly and thoroughly damp, but avoid standing water; feed every four weeks until August; tolerates some frost (to about 23 °F (-5 °C)), can be brought indoors in late fall and put back outdoors in April; winter over in a bright, barely frost-free 36–41 °F (2–5 °C) place, keeping slightly damp
Propagation: From cuttings in spring and summer
Design: Very attractive ornamental foliage plant for shady places, with hosta, fuchsia, astilbe, and ferns as neighbors; also pretty as decorative plant at entrance to house or patio

Height:
*3–10 ft
(1–3 m)*
Bloom Time:
*not
applicable*

*evergreen
shrubs*

Bambusoidae (Subfamily)

Bamboo

Family: Grasses (Poaceae or Graminae)
Origin: East Asia
Description: Flowers appear only every couple of decades, after blooming the plants usually die back; growth: stiffly erect or broad and bushy, in some cases trailing; lanceolate, usually large leaves, often with decoratively colored blades
Location: Preferably partial shade, but also sunny (not full sun); protected from wind if possible
Care: Keep evenly and thoroughly damp, but avoid standing water at all costs; feed every four weeks until end of July; winter over in a bright place at 41–50 °F (5–10 °C); water sparingly but keep air humidity high; cut out older stalks in spring
Propagation: By division in spring
Design: Lends itself to use as a visual screen
Species/Cultivars: Suitable for container culture are cultivars of umbrella bamboo (*Fargesia murielae*), as well as various *Phyllostachus* species and cultivars and golden bamboo (*Pleioblastus auricoma*).

Height:
*3–10 ft
(1–3 m)*
Bloom Time:
*April/June–
September*

*deciduous
climbing
shrub*

Bougainvillea Species and Hybrids

Bougainvillea

Family: Bougainvillea (Nyctaginaceae)
Origin: Brazil
Description: Small, white flowers; luxuriant "bloom" produced by strikingly colored bracts, in *B. glabra* lilac or white, in *B. spectabilis* as well as *B.* hybrids also yellow, orange, or red; growth: erect or climbing with long, wood-forming, thorn-covered shoots
Location: Sunny, also full sun; warm place, protected from rain and wind
Care: On hot days, water abundantly but avoid standing water; feed weekly until August; train upward by using sturdy stakes in pot or climbing frame; winter over in a bright place at 46–54 °F (8–12 °C), cut back before bringing indoors
Propagation: From cuttings taken from new growth in spring, though it is difficult, as they do not take root easily in some cases
Design: Especially effective in an exposed place without overly eye-catching neighbors; suitable companions are marguerite daisies and true myrtle, for example

Height:
*3–10 ft
(1–3 m)*
Bloom Time:
*July–
September*

*deciduous
shrub/tree*

Brugmansia Species and Hybrids
Angel's Trumpet

Family: Nightshade (Solanaceae)
Origin: South America
Description: Funnel-shaped hanging flowers, 10–20 in.
(25–50 cm) long, white, pink, yellow, orange, or red, intensely
scented in evening; growth: usually shrubby, broad, and bushy
Location: Sunny to partial shade; warm, protected from wind
Care: In summer, drench completely; feed weekly until
August; deadhead and remove faded leaves regularly; frequent
repotting recommended; winter over in a light or dark place
at 39–54 °F (4–12 °C), the cooler it is, the less light is
required; cut back before bringing indoors, especially if wintered over in a dark spot
Propagation: From cuttings, from spring to fall
Design: Decorative container plant with lush, tropical look;
needs plenty of space, visually as well as physically, to unfold
its beauty
Tip: All the parts are highly toxic! The plants can cause skin
irritations in sensitive persons, and their scent can produce
headaches and nausea.

Height:
1–3 ft
(0.3–1 m)
Bloom Time:
April–May

*evergreen
small shrub*

Buxus sempervirens 'Suffruticosa'

Boxwood

Family: Box (Buxaceae)
Origin: Southern and Western Europe
Description: Flowers yellowish green or whitish green, inconspicuous, but scented; growth: dense, bushy, slow; tiny, ovate, shiny dark-green leaves
Location: Sunny to shade
Care: Keep moderately damp; until mid-August feed every four weeks; tolerates cutting well; best time to prune: late May and August; winter over outdoors, in harsh sites with winter protection
Propagation: From cuttings in early summer
Design: Depending on your taste, you can simply let boxwood grow, or shape it regularly; this is simple with round or pyramidal forms, which you initially should create by using homemade wire templates. Spheres of boxwood are very effective in "pairs," for example, to the left and right of the balcony door.

Height:
*3–8 ft
(1–2.5 m)*
Bloom Time:
May–July

*evergreen
shrub*

Callistemon citrinus

Crimson Bottlebrush

Family: Myrtle (Myrtaceae)
Origin: Australia
Description: Flowers with long red filaments, tightly clustered in large erect inflorescences resembling bottle brushes; growth: bushy to stiffly erect, quite fast-growing, individual shoots often tower above the flowers; long, leathery, lanceolate leaves
Location: Sunny, also full sun
Care: Water generously, with soft water if possible; feed lime-poor fertilizer, such as rhododendron food, every two weeks; trim shoots of younger plants often to promote bushy growth; pot in acid potting mix (rhododendron soil); winter over in a bright place at 41–50 °F (5–10 °C), also somewhat darker if necessary
Propagation: From semilignified tip cuttings in late summer; pinch back young plants several times
Design: Fits well with Mediterranean container plants; pretty, for example, with true myrtle

Height:
3–6 ft
(1–2 m)
Bloom Time:
January–
April

evergreen
shrub

Camellia Species and Hybrids
Camellia

Family: Camellia (Theaceae)
Origin: East Asia
Description: Flowers in pink, red, or white, single, semidouble, or double, up to 4.5 in. (12 cm) across; bushy growth, in some cases with overhanging shoots; broad, ovate, shiny dark-green leaves
Location: Partial shade or bright place, but no blazing sun; protected from wind and rain
Care: Keep moderately damp, use soft water; add rhododendron food weekly; once buds appear (around late July), water less and stop feeding; spray frequently; pot in rhododendron soil; bring indoors before first frost and put in a bright place, cool (about 41 °F (5 °C)) until flowers open, keep at 50–59 °F (10–15 °C) during bloom, water sparingly
Propagation: From tip cuttings in summer
Design: Blooms best and earliest in conservatory; in summer, attractive foliage plant

Height:
*up to 10 ft
(3 m)*
Bloom Time:
*July–
September*

*deciduous
climbing
shrub*

Campsis radicans

Trumpet Creeper

Family: Trumpet creeper (Bignoniaceae)
Origin: North America
Description: Funnel-shaped flowers up to 3 in. (8 cm) long, orange, red, or yellow, in umbel-like inflorescences; climbs with holdfasts, also slightly twining, with enough room it reaches a height of 16 ft (5 m) and more; attractively pinnate leaves
Location: Sunny; if possible, warm and somewhat protected from wind
Care: Keep moderately damp; supply slow-release fertilizer in spring, if necessary add more in July; trim withered shoots to two to four eyes in late summer or early spring; needs climbing frame only after reaching height of 6 ft (2 m); winter over outdoors with winter protection, cut back frozen shoots in spring
Propagation: Not possible with cultivars (grafted)
Design: Especially suitable to enhance facades, looks particularly lovely in front of a white wall; in a roomy container, very pretty with ground morning glory as underplanting

Height:
*1–4.9 ft
(0.3–1.5 m)*
Bloom Time:
*June–
October*

*herbaceous
perennial,
not winter
hardy*

Canna indica Hybrids
Indian Shot

Family: Canna (Cannaceae)
Origin: Western India, Central and South America, Africa
Description: Flowers red, orange, pink, yellow, white, also bicolored, about 4 in. (10 cm) long; grows in broad rosettes composed of large, erect leaves, bright green or blue-green, reddish, or bronze in color
Location: Preferably full sun
Care: Water copiously in summer, but avoid standing water; feed weekly until August; deadhead regularly; cut back shoots to a hand's width after the first frost, remove the tuberous rhizomes, let them dry, lay them in peat or sand, keep in a dark place at 41–50 °F (5–10 °C), plant in March, then put in a warm and bright place
Propagation: By division of the rhizomes in spring
Design: Very attractive in combinations of different cultivars in various colors; low cultivars also for balcony boxes and large bowls

C

Height:
20–40 in.
(0.5–1 m)
Bloom Time:
August–
October

deciduous
small shrub

Caryopteris x clandonensis

Bluebeard

Family: Verbena (Verbenaceae)
Origin: East Asia
Description: Flowers blue to bluish violet, small and densely packed in panicles; erect growth with numerous shoots; lanceolate leaves, with gray, felt-like covering underneath
Location: Sunny; somewhat protected
Care: Keep moderately damp, avoid standing water at all costs; feed every two weeks until August; can be trimmed substantially in spring; winter over in light or dark place, at 41–50 °F (5–10 °C), or even outdoors with good protection, cut out frozen shoots in spring
Propagation: From cuttings in summer
Design: Marvelous fall bloomer, can be accompanied by small pots containing heather and broom or bushy aster; also pretty next to yellow or red fall chrysanthemums
Species/Cultivars: Reliable cultivars are 'Heavenly Blue' (light violet blue) and 'Kew Blue' (dark blue-violet).

Height:
*3–6.5 ft
(1–2 m)*
Bloom Time:
*May–
September*

*evergreen
shrub*

Cestrum elegans
Red Cestrum

Family: Nightshade (Solanaceae)
Origin: Mexico
Description: Flowers purplish red, tube-shaped, in dense, hanging racemes; growth: bushy, with relatively thin shoots, some overhanging; fast-growing
Location: Sunny
Care: Water abundantly in summer; feed weekly, stake shoots if necessary or tie to trellis; thin out occasionally; winter over in a bright place at 41–50 °F (5–10 °C) and then blooming will start in spring, or in a dark place at about 41 °F (5 °C), cutting back shoots to a hand's breadth in fall and keeping almost dry
Propagation: From cuttings in spring
Design: Especially lovely as a standard, pretty in small groups with other South American plants such as angel's trumpet, Argentine senna, century plant
Species/Cultivars: Quite commonly, *C. aurantiacum* also is available with yellowish orange flowers.

Height:
3–10 ft
(1–3 m)
Bloom Time:
March–June

evergreen
rosette-tree

Chamaerops humilis
Dwarf Fan Palm

Family: Palm (Arecaceae)
Origin: Mediterranean region
Description: Yellow-green flowers, rare in container culture; multiple trunks, with dense, fan-like palm fronds over 20 in. (50 cm) wide, blue-green in color, with spiny stems
Location: Preferably full sun, also light shade; protected from rain if at all possible
Care: Keep evenly damp; feed weekly until August; repotting seldom necessary; tolerates light frost, can be brought indoors late and taken back out early; ideally, winter over in a bright place at about 41 °F (5 °C), if need be also in a dark place, or in a very bright spot but somewhat warmer (up to 59 °F (15 °C)), water sparingly
Propagation: By division in spring or from seed, which is difficult
Design: Very attractive palm for containers, highly decorative even without blooming neighbors; needs lots of room, as it grows wide; on large patios, pretty with oleander and bougainvillea

Height:
*20–60 in.
(0.5–1.5 m)*
Bloom Time:
May–July

*evergreen
shrub*

Cistus creticus

Pink Rockrose

Family: Rockrose (Cistaceae)
Origin: Southern Europe, North Africa
Description: Flowers bright pink, large, saucer-shaped, slightly wrinkled in appearance, individual flowers last only a short while but are constantly replaced by new ones; growth: bushy, erect, with gray-green leaves
Location: Full sun; warm
Care: Water amply in summer, but avoid standing water; cut back by at least 1/3 right after the bloom in summer and keep drier; until August feed every two weeks; winter over in a bright place at 41–50 °F (5–10 °C)
Propagation: From tip cuttings in summer or from seed in spring; pinch back young plants several times
Design: Fits very well in Mediterranean designs, for example, with olive and lavender
Species/Cultivars: Other frequently available species are *C. ladanifer* (white flowers with reddish-brown flecks), *C. x purpureus* (pink), and *C. salviifolius* (white).

Height:
20–60 in.
(0.5–1.5 m)
Bloom Time:
March–
August

evergreen
shrub

x Citrofortunella microcarpa

Calamondin Orange

Other Name: Botanically, also *C. mitis*
Family: Citrus fruit (Rutaceae)
Origin: Cross between tangerine (*Citrus reticulate*) and kumquat (*Fortunella margarita* → page 157)
Description: Flowers white, star-shaped, scented; in conservatory blooms almost year-round; tangerine-like fruits, orange in color when ripe, edible, but quite bland; bushy growth; leathery, glossy dark-green leaves
Location: Sunny; warm, protected from wind and rain
Care: Keep moist but not wet; feed weekly until August; if possible, use only soft water, citrus substrate, and special citrus food; winter over in a bright place at 39–46 °F (4–8 °C), water sparingly, ventilate often
Propagation: From cuttings in spring and summer
Design: Pretty in container plant arrangements with a Mediterranean as well as Asian air
Tip: The plant is very similar to the *Citrus* species (→ page 144) but more robust and easier to cultivate.

Height:
*20–60 in.
(0.5–1.5 m)*
Bloom Time:
*March–
August*

*evergreen
shrub/tree*

Citrus Species

Citrus Standard

Family: Citrus (Rutaceae)
Origin: East Asia, Southeast Asia
Description: Flowers white, more rarely pink, star-shaped, scented, in a conservatory appearing almost year-round; depending on species, yellow or orange fruit, edible, but often sour; growth: bushy; leathery, glossy dark-green leaves
Location: Sunny; warm, protected from wind and rain
Care: As for calamondin orange (→ page 143); the *Citrus* species, however, are somewhat more sensitive to wet as well as to root-ball dryness, and less tolerant of cold; in fall, bring indoors early and place outdoors again only in late May; winter over as for calamondin orange
Propagation: From cuttings in spring and summer
Design: Available and/or trainable as standards, but often have a more harmonious effect in bush form
Species/Cultivars: Numerous species, such as lemon (*C. limon*), orange (*C. sinensis*), and the daintier tangerine (*C. reticulata*); also similar is the kumquat (→ page 157)

Height:
*up to 10 ft
(3 m)*
Bloom Time:
*May–June/
September*

*deciduous
climbing
shrub*

Clematis Hybrids

Clematis (Early-Blooming)

Family: Buttercup (Ranunculaceae)
Origin: East Asia and Europe
Description: Flowers in many colors, large, usually plate-shaped, main bloom in early summer, second bloom in August/September; twining climber; pinnate leaves
Location: Sunny to partial shade
Care: Keep evenly damp; provide slow-release fertilizer in spring, add more in July; winter over outdoors with winter protection; cut back lightly in late fall or spring, trim shoots by about 8 in. (20 cm)
Propagation: Not applicable, as it is grafted
Design: Attractive climber for pergolas, trellises, and facades
Species/Cultivars: Pretty cultivars are, for example, 'Lasurstern' (blue flowers), 'Mme. Le Coultre' (white), 'Nelly Moser' (light pink with darker stripes), 'The President' (dark blue-violet); for late-blooming hybrids → page 146
Tip: The plants contain skin irritants.

Height:
*up to 10 ft
(3 m)*
Bloom Time:
*June/July–
September*

*deciduous
climbing
shrub*

Clematis Hybrids

Clematis (Late-Blooming)

Family: Buttercup (Ranunculaceae)
Origin: East Asia and Europe
Description: Flowers in many colors, also multicolored, large, usually plate-shaped, single or double; twining climber; pinnate leaves
Location: Sunny to partial shade
Care: As for early-blooming clematis (→ page 145), but cut in late winter or early spring, making sure to cut back vigorously (to 8–20 in. (20–50 cm))
Propagation: Not applicable, as it is grafted
Design: In front of a flowering wall of clematis, yellow-blooming container plants or potted woody plants like hibiscus or cinquefoil are especially beautiful.
Species/Cultivars: Pretty cultivars especially suitable for container cultivation are 'Ernest Markham' (magenta), 'Jackmanii' (dark violet), 'Rhapsody' (blue), 'Rütel' (dark red), 'Ville de Lyon' (crimson)
Tip: The plants contain skin irritants.

Height:
*3–10 ft
(1–3 m)*
Bloom Time:
May–June

*evergreen
tree*

Cupressus macrocarpa

Monterey Cypress

Family: Cypress (Cupressaceae)
Origin: California
Description: Flowers greenish yellow, inconspicuous, rare in pot culture; growth: slender, erect, with scale-shaped, bright-green needles; the widespread cultivar 'Gold rest' has golden yellow needles
Location: Bright, but not in blazing sun, to partial shade; if possible, somewhat protected from wind
Care: Keep evenly and slightly damp; feed every three to four weeks until August; tolerates pruning; tolerates some frost, can be brought indoors late; winter over in a bright place at 41–50 °F (5–10 °C), in winter quarters water occasionally, but do not keep overly damp
Design: Pretty companion for flowering container plants, but can hold its own alone as well
Species/Cultivars: Another species suitable for container culture is the Mediterranean cypress (*C. sempervirens* var. *sempervirens*), which is similar in description and needs.

Height:
*3–6.5 ft
(1–2 m)*
Bloom Time:
*not
applicable*

*evergreen
rosette-tree*

Cycas revoluta
Sago Palm

Family: Cycad (Cycadaceae)
Origin: Southern Japan
Description: Flowers only on older specimens, like conifers; growth: broad, clump-like, with dense, long, slightly pendent, fern-like pinnate fronds; the plant grows very slowly
Location: Best in partial shade, also shade; protected from rain
Care: Do not water until top layer of soil is dried out, but don't let root-ball dry out completely; feed lightly every four weeks until August; tolerates light frost for a short time, winter over in a bright place at 54–59 °F (12–15 °C), keep almost dry
Propagation: Possible from seeds, but time-consuming and difficult
Design: Splendid backdrop for container plants and potted woody plants with showy blooms; attractive ornamental foliage plant for shady areas

Height:
*1–2 ft
(0.3–0.6 m)*
Bloom Time:
*depending
on species,
April–July*

*deciduous
small
shrubs*

Cytisus, Chamaecytisus, Genista

Broom

Family: Legume (Fabaceae)
Origin: Central and Southern Europe
Description: Flowers yellow, in *C. purpureus* purplish pink to violet; growth: bushy or creeping
Location: Sunny
Care: Keep only slightly damp; feed little; if bloom diminishes, cut back part of the shoots; winter over outdoors with winter protection
Propagation: From cuttings
Design: For wide pots or troughs, pretty with herbaceous plants as underplanting
Species/Cultivars: Especially suitable for containers are the creeping to prostrate species of *Cytisus,* such as prostrate broom (*C. decumbens;* yellow flowers), dwarf broom (*C. x beanii;* yellow), Kew broom (*C. x kewensis*), Lydia broom (*Genista lydia;* yellow), and the bushy, quite low purple broom (*Chamaecytisus purpureus;* purple).

Height:
*6–10 ft
(2–3 m)*
Bloom Time:
*not
applicable*

*evergreen
large
herbaceous
perennial*

Ensete ventricosum

Abyssinian Banana

Family: Banana (Musaceae)
Origin: South and East Africa
Description: Flowers yellowish, very rarely seen in container culture; palm-like growth habit with hollow false stem; broad, oval leaves up to 10 ft (3 m) long, some with red central rib
Location: Sunny (also full sun) to partial shade; protected from wind, if possible
Care: Needs lots of water, keep evenly damp, but not wet; feed weekly until August; winter over in as bright a place as possible, at 50–59 °F (10–15 °C); if winter quarters are light–poor, cut back to leaves of heart before bringing indoors and keep at 50 °F (10 °C), water sparingly, but don't pour water into the "heart" or the plant will die
Propagation: From seed, January–April, at 68–77 °F (20–25 °C)
Design: Impressive foliage plant with a tropical flair, to use alone or as a backdrop for species with showy flowers; wonderful on large patios with angel's trumpet, Paraguay nightshade, or Port St. Johns creeper

Height:
*5–10 ft
(1.5–3 m)*
Bloom Time:
*September–
November*

*evergreen
tree/shrub*

Eriobotrya japonica

Loquat

Other Name: Japanese plum
Family: Rose (Rosaceae)
Origin: China, Japan
Description: Small, white, scented flowers in panicles, from which yellow-orange fruit develops in spring; regular display of flowers and fruit only in conservatory; growth: bushy and branching; longish, ovate, shiny dark-green leaves up to 1 ft (30 cm) long, grayish white to reddish and "woolly" beneath
Location: Sunny to partial shade; protect from rain
Care: Keep moderately damp; feed every two weeks; tolerates some frost, can be brought indoors late; winter over in a bright place at about 50 °F (10 °C), somewhat warmer if necessary, or in a dark place at 41 °F (5 °C), but then keep almost dry
Propagation: Year-round from seeds or—more difficult—from cuttings of green wood
Design: With its dark foliage, it allows bloomers placed in front of it to shine

Height:
3–6.5 ft
(1–2 m)
Bloom Time:
July–
September

deciduous
shrub

Erythrina crista-galli

Cockspur Coral Tree

Family: Legume (Fabaceae)
Origin: South America
Description: Large, bright coral-red papilionaceous flowers in long, sometimes pendulous racemes; growth: bushy, loosely structured, shoots often have thorns; lovely pinnate foliage
Location: Sunny, also full sun
Care: Water copiously in summer; feed every two weeks until August; winter over in a dark place at 41–46 °F (5–8 °C), before bringing indoors cut the drying shoots close to the stem or to four eyes, in spring put in a brighter, warmer place once new growth begins, and water
Propagation: From cuttings or from seed in spring
Design: Contributes to an air of tropical beauty in combination with other "South Americans," such as angel's trumpet, Argentine senna, or Spanish bayonet, in summers with good weather; also goes well with palms
Tip: With good care, cockspur coral tree will bloom more luxuriantly every year, unless the summer is rainy.

Height:
*6–10 ft
(2–3 m)*
Bloom Time:
varies

*evergreen
tree*

Eucalyptus Species

Eucalyptus

Family: Myrtle (Myrtaceae)
Origin: Australia
Description: Flowers of *E. ficifolia* in summer, bunches of red filaments; of *E. gunnii* in fall, cream-colored; of other species, rare in container culture; growth habit: single-stemmed or bushy and branching, with gray-green leaves that are aromatic when rubbed
Location: Full sun to partial shade
Care: Water generously in summer, but avoid standing water if at all possible; feed only occasionally; winter over in a bright place at 41–50 °F (5–10 °C), older plants tolerate light frost
Propagation: From seed in spring (light germinator)
Design: Very pretty as background for blooming container plants and potted woody plants
Species/Cultivars: Slow-growing: *E. gunnii* (silvery blue leaves, round at first, later lanceolate) and *E. citriodora* (lance-olate leaves with lemon scent); fast-growing: *E. globulus* (blue gum) and *E. ficifolia*

Height:
*1–3 ft
(0.3–1 m)*
Bloom Time:
*May–
October*

*evergreen
semishrub*

Euryops chrysanthemoides

Daisy Bush

Other Name: Bull's eye
Family: Aster, daisy, or sunflower (Asteraceae)
Origin: South Africa
Description: Yellow, long-stemmed daisy-like flowers with orange-yellow center; growth: bushy and branching, with heavily pinnate dark-green leaves
Location: Sunny, also full sun
Care: Keep evenly damp; feed every two weeks until August; cut out withered stalks regularly; can be shaped in spring by cutting back (by about 1/3 to 1/2); winter over in a bright place at 41–50 °F (5–10 °C)
Propagation: From semiripe tip cuttings in summer
Design: Adds color to groups of container plants; can also be used on the balcony owing to its modest height; pretty companion for bright pink or red roses in pots, most beautiful with lavender
Tip: Very similar to the usually white-blooming marguerite daisy (→ page 129)

Height:
*10–20 ft
(3–6 m)*
Bloom Time:
*July–
October*

*deciduous
climbing
shrub*

Fallopia baldschuanica

Russian Vine

Other Names: Silver lace vine; often known under the previous botanical name, *F. aubertii*
Family: Smartweed or buckwheat (Polygonaceae)
Origin: Central Asia
Description: Flowers white to delicate pink, small, in long, hanging panicles, scented; fast-growing twining plant; heart-shaped leaves
Location: Sunny to partial shade; also in shade, though it will not bloom luxuriantly
Care: Water amply in summer, but don't keep constantly wet; feed every two weeks until August; very stable climbing support needed; thin out in spring, radical cutting back possible and advisable every three to five years; regularly trim to keep rain gutters and the like clear; winter over outdoors with winter protection
Propagation: From cuttings
Design: Quickly adds attractive green element to facades, climbing supports, fences, and pergolas.

Height:
3–8 ft
(1–2.5 m)
Bloom Time:
(May)–
September

deciduous
tree

Ficus carica

Common Fig

Other Name: Fig tree
Family: Mulberry (Moraceae)
Origin: Southwestern Asia, Southern Europe
Description: Pitcher-shaped (urceolate) inflorescences, from which fruit develops under favorable conditions in spring or late summer; growth: shrubby or short-stemmed with broad crown; large, bright-green, multilobed, leathery leaves
Location: Sunny; somewhat protected
Care: Water abundantly in summer; feed weekly until August; can be cut back in fall; winter over in a bright place if possible, in a dark one if necessary, at 36–46 °F (2–8 °C); tolerates some frost, bring indoors late and take back out in April, first placing it in light shade
Propagation: From tip cuttings taken in late summer or spring
Design: Provides Mediterranean flair; very pretty, for example, with oleander, rosemary, and lavender; also effective alone as a highly decorative foliage plant

Height:
3–5 ft
(1–1.5 m)
Bloom Time:
March–
August

evergreen
shrub/tree

Fortunella margarita

Kumquat

Family: Citrus fruit (Rutaceae)
Origin: Southern China
Description: Flowers white, star-shaped, slightly scented, appearing almost year-round in conservatory; oval fruit, orange when ripe, with good, fruity taste; growth: bushy, with thorny shoots and leathery leaves
Location: Sunny; somewhat protected from wind and rain
Care: Keep damp but not wet; feed weekly until August; use only soft water, citrus substrate, and special citrus food, if possible; provide support for larger plants; winter over in a bright place at 39–46 °F (4–8 °C), water sparingly, ventilate frequently on frost-free days
Propagation: From cuttings in spring and summer, or from seed (easier)
Design: Goes well in groups with an Asian air, including bamboo and hibiscus
Tip: Kumquat seems like a robust version of the closely related *Citrus* species (→ page 144).

Height:
1.5–6.5 ft
(0.5–2 m)
Bloom Time:
May–
October

deciduous
shrub

Fuchsia Hybrids
Fuchsia

Family: Evening primrose (Onagraceae)
Origin: South and Central America, New Zealand
Description: Funnel-shaped bell flowers in red, pink, white, blue-violet, often bicolored, single, semidouble, or double, in racemes or panicles; growth: bushy or with overhanging shoots as a standard
Location: Preferably partial shade, or bright place without direct sun, also shade; protected from wind
Care: Keep evenly damp; feed weekly until August; deadhead; winter over in a bright or a dark place at 43–46 °F (6–8 °C), if dark, then somewhat cooler; cut back in spring if necessary, trim vigorous early spring shoots to one to three buds
Propagation: From cuttings taken in spring or late summer
Design: Especially charming as a standard
Tip: Low fuchsia cultivars are suitable for balcony boxes (→ page 67).

Height:
*18 to 30 in.
(0.5–0.8 m)*
Bloom Time:
May–June

*evergreen
small shrub*

Gaultheria mucronata
Prickly Heath

Other Name: Botanically, also *Pernettya mucronata*
Family: Heather (Ericaceae)
Origin: Chile
Description: Flowers whitish to pink, pitcher-shaped; from August on, numerous spherical berries, depending on cultivar red, pink, or white, long-lasting, slightly toxic like all other plant parts; growth: broad and bushy, erect; shiny dark-green leaves
Location: Partial shade to shade
Care: Sensitive to lime, so plant in rhododendron soil mixed with sand; keep only slightly damp with soft water; feed every two months until August (rhododendron food); cutting back every two or three years promotes compact growth; winter over outdoors with good protection, in sites exposed to harsh weather better indoors in a bright place at 41–50 °F (5–10 °C)
Propagation: From cuttings
Design: As a young plant, often used in mixed winter boxes, for example, with dwarf conifers

Height:
*up to 8 in.
(0.2 m)*
Bloom Time:
June–July

*evergreen
dwarf shrub*

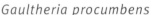

Gaultheria procumbens

Wintergreen

Other Names: Checkerberry, boxberry
Family: Heather (Ericaceae)
Origin: Canada, North America
Description: White to light pink, pitcher-shaped flowers; from
September on, red, spherical berries, long-lasting, slightly
toxic like the rest of the plant; growth: clump-like, flat, and
spreading; glossy dark-green leaves, reddish bronze in color in
winter
Location: Partial shade to shade
Care: Sensitive to lime, needs rhododendron soil (mixed with
sand) and food, soft water or rainwater; keep only slightly
damp; feed every two months until August; limit cutting to
removal of awkward shoots; winter over outdoors, protect
from heavy frost (root area)
Propagation: By division or from seed in spring
Design: Decorative partner for dwarf conifers and winter
heath in fall and winter plantings, as young plant also in
mixed boxes

Height:
4–8 in.
(0.3–0.6 m)
Bloom Time:
August–September

evergreen shrub

Hebe x andersonii

Anderson's Hawksbeard

Family: Figwort (Scrophulariaceae)
Origin: New Zealand
Description: Small tubular flowers in blue-violet, red, or white, in ears or racemes; growth: bushy; narrow, ovate or rounded, glossy dark-green, leathery leaves, in the cultivar 'Variegata' with light spots
Location: Preferably bright place, but not in blazing sun; somewhat protected from wind and rain
Care: Keep evenly damp, but avoid standing water; until August, feed lightly every two weeks; if necessary, thin out in spring by removing or cutting back older shoots; winter over in a bright place, at 46–50 °F (8–10 °C)
Propagation: From tip cuttings in summer; pinch back young plants several times
Design: Pretty in combinations with dusty miller, heather, autumn crocus, or evergreen dwarf woody plants, in containers and large boxes; provides ornamental foliage all summer long

Height:
up to 16 ft
(5 m)
Bloom Time:
September

evergreen
climbing
shrub

Hedera helix

Ivy

Family: Ivy (Araliaceae)
Origin: Western and Central Europe
Description: Flowers yellow-green, only on older specimens,
developing into black berries (highly toxic!); climbs with
suckers, also grows creeping or hanging; three- to five-lobed
juvenile leaves, diamond-shaped mature leaves, cultivars with
light-patterned foliage
Location: Sunny to shade
Care: Keep moderately damp; add slow-release fertilizer in
April/May; cutting back possible, best in late July; winter over
outdoors with winter protection
Propagation: From cuttings taken from young shoots with
suckers
Design: Especially valuable for shady places; young plants also
in boxes and hanging planters
Tip: Be careful, the suckers can damage facades if the stucco
or mortar is not intact; better to provide a climbing frame.

Height:
3–6 ft
(1–2 m)
Bloom Time:
March–
October

evergreen
shrub

Hibiscus rosa-sinensis
Chinese Hibiscus

Family: Mallow (Malvaceae)
Origin: East Asia
Description: Large, funnel-like flowers in yellow, orange, red, pink, or white, with long stamen column, single or double; growth: broad and bushy; shiny dark-green leaves
Location: Bright place, but no blazing midday sun; protected from wind and rain
Care: Keep damp, but avoid standing water at all costs; feed weekly until August; remove faded blooms and leaves; provide support for standard; cut back older specimens by about half in spring; winter over in a bright place at 54–61 °F (12–16 °C), water with restraint
Propagation: From cuttings in May
Design: Very attractive both as bush and as standard
Tip: Shift around as little as possible, as it reacts to frequent change of location, as well as to very uneven watering, by dropping buds

Height:
*up to 16 ft
(5 m)*
Bloom Time:
June–July

*deciduous
climbing
shrub*

Hydrangea anomala ssp. petiolaris

Climbing Hydrangea

Family: Hydrangea (Hydrangaceae)
Origin: East Asia
Description: White flowers in umbrella-like corymbs up to 8 in. (20 cm) across, appearing at earliest two years after planting; climbs by means of suckers, growing slowly at first and speeding up noticeably from the third year on; heart-shaped, glossy green leaves
Location: Best in partial shade, also in shade or in a bright place without blazing midday sun
Care: Keep damp at all times, water with soft water; feed every two weeks until August; remove overmature shoots after bloom; cutting back not essential, but possible if needed; climbing aid recommended despite suckers; winter over outdoors, protect root area in case of hard frost
Propagation: From cuttings in summer
Design: Very attractive on walls and pergolas, with beautiful decorative foliage even when not in bloom

Height:
*20–60 in.
(0.5–1.5 m)*
Bloom Time:
May–July

*deciduous
shrub*

Hydrangea macrophylla

French Hydrangea

Other Name: Bigleaf hydrangea
Family: Hydrangea (Hydrangaceae)
Origin: Japan, Korea
Description: Hemispheric, ball-shaped or plate-shaped inflorescences in pink, red, blue, or white; *H.* hybrids bloom until September; growth: broad and bushy, erect
Location: Partial shade
Care: Keep well dampened but not wet, use only soft water; supply rhododendron food every two weeks until August; remove withered blooms regularly; pot in rhododendron soil; winter over in a light or dark place at 36–46 °F (2–8 °C); tolerates some frost
Propagation: From cuttings in early summer
Design: Striking bloomer for partial shade, depending on container and companions has an elegant effect or a rustic country look
Tip: The coloring of the blooms also depends on the acidity of the soil; blue, if the soil is very acid, pink, if the acidity is low

Height:
3–6.5 ft
(1–2 m)
Bloom Time:
May–
October

semiever-
green shrub

Iochroma cyaneum
Violet Churur

Family: Nightshade (Solanaceae)
Origin: Central and South America
Description: Flowers violet, blue, or red, narrow, long tubes in bunches; growth: somewhat leggy, little branching, with long, quite brittle shoots; large, narrow, elliptical bright-green leaves that are shed in cool winter temperatures
Location: Sunny to partial shade; protect from wind
Care: Keep evenly and thoroughly damp; feed weekly until August; guide shoots with stakes or framework; pinch back young plants; winter over in a light or dark place at 41–54 °F (5–12 °C), cut back before bringing it indoors or in March; if leaves drop, keep almost dry all winter
Propagation: From herbaceous cuttings in summer
Design: Handsome as a standard; good in groups with other tropical plants such as Argentine senna, angel's trumpet, canna, or palms; can also be trained to grow up a trellis on the house wall

Height:
1.5–8 ft
(0.5–2.5 m)
Bloom Time:
depends on
species

shrubs,
usually
evergreen

Jasminum Species

Jasmine

Family: Olive (Oleaceae)
Origin: East Asia
Description: Flowers white or yellow, tubular, often intensely scented; growth: twining and climbing, with long, thin shoots, quite fast-growing; glossy green ovate or round leaves, in some cases pinnate
Location: Sunny, but not blazing midday sun, or partial shade; somewhat protected from wind and rain
Care: Keep evenly damp; feed every two weeks; cutting back quite possible; repot often; winter over most species in a bright place at 41–50 °F (5–10 °C)
Propagation: From semiripe cuttings in summer
Design: Climbing plants with a marvelous scent
Species/Cultivars: Numerous species are occasionally available; most common are *J. mesnyi* (yellow flowers in March–May, second bloom in summer) and *J. polyanthum* (white, May–August/September); see also winter jasmine (→ page 168)

Height:
*3–10 ft
(1–3 m)*
Bloom Time:
*January–
March/
April*

*deciduous,
long-
stemmed
shrub*

Jasminum nudiflorum
Winter Jasmine

Family: Olive (Oleaceae)
Origin: Western China
Description: Flowers yellow, star-shaped, appearing before the leaf flush; growth: climbing as a rambler (the cane-like shoots spread out on a suitable surface), otherwise pendent; dark-green leaves
Location: Best in bright place, but protected from intense late-winter sun, also in partial shade
Care: Keep moderately damp; apply slow-release fertilizer after bloom; tie up shoots; every two or three years thin out by cutting out older shoots after the bloom; winter over outdoors, protect root area in heavy frost
Propagation: From cuttings in summer
Design: An unusual treat in winter with its bright yellow flowers on bare branches; truly delightful when underplanted with small spring bloomers like crocus, snowdrops, and Siberian squill; you can plant the bulbs in the container as early as fall

Height:
8–40 in.
(0.2–1 m)
Bloom Time:
not
applicable

evergreen
conifer

Juniperus Species in Cultivars

Dwarf Juniper

Family: Cypress (Cupressaceae)
Origin: Europe, East Asia
Description: Columnar to flat, spreading growth; narrow, sharp needles
Location: Sun
Care: Keep evenly damp; apply slow-release fertilizer in spring, add more conifer food in June/July for larger specimens; winter over outdoors, protect root area well in case of heavy frost
Propagation: Not applicable, as it is often grafted
Design: Good for breaking up little groups of blooming container plants in summer; pretty conifers for winter and long-term plantings
Species/Cultivars: Selection: *J. chinensis* 'Plumosa Aurea' (bushy, with yellow needles), *J. communis* 'Meyer' (columnar, silvery green), 'Repanda' (wide and cushion-like, silvery green), *J. procumbens* 'Nana' (cushion-like, blue-green), *J. squamata* 'Blue Star' (broad and rounded, silvery blue)

Height:
*3–10 ft
(1–3 m)*
Bloom Time:
*late July–
October*

*deciduous
shrub/
tree*

Lagerstroemia indica

Crape Myrtle

Other Name: Chinese crape myrtle
Family: Loosestrife (Lythraceae)
Origin: China, Korea
Description: Flowers pink, red, or white, in conical, lilac-like panicles; growth: erect, with sturdy shoots; ovate, dark-green leaves
Location: Full sun; if possible, warm, somewhat protected
Care: Keep evenly damp, buds will drop if root-ball dries out; feed every three or four weeks; cut back heavily in fall and thin out; tolerates some frost, can be brought indoors late; winter over in a dark place at 39–46 °F (4–8 °C) and keep almost dry; in spring, put in a bright, warmer spot
Propagation: From seed or from semiripe tip cuttings in summer
Design: Very appealing as a standard, but also attractive in bush form; reserve enough room, as it grows quite broad; as a standard, it can be nicely underplanted with lobelia or sweet alyssum

Height:
*1–5 ft
(0.3–1.5 m)*
Bloom Time:
*June–
October*

*evergreen
shrub*

Lantana camara

Lantana

Family: Verbena (Verbenaceae)
Origin: Central and South America
Description: Flowers in compound umbels, usually changing color, for example, from pink to red or yellow to orange; also cultivars with white, pink, or violet flowers, some with yellow eye; bushy growth, with some overhanging flower shoots; ovate, dark-green, wrinkled leaves
Location: Sunny
Care: Keep evenly damp; feed every two weeks until August; deadhead regularly, also remove the green berries if they appear; tolerates cutting well; winter over in a bright place, after cutting back in fall also in a dark place, at 43–50 °F (6–10 °C), keep almost dry, cut back shoots by half before bringing indoors or in spring
Propagation: From cuttings in spring
Design: Very charming as a standard; yellow-red cultivars pretty next to blue-violet Paraguay nightshade; young plants also suitable for balcony boxes

Height:
*3–6.5 ft
(1–2 m)*
Bloom Time:
April–May

*evergreen
shrub/
tree*

Laurus nobilis

Bay Laurel Tree

Family: Laurel (Lauraceae)
Origin: Mediterranean region
Description: Flowers greenish yellow, inconspicuous; growth: erect, dense, and bushy, slow-growing; elliptical, dark-green, glossy, leathery leaves
Location: Prefers sunny, but also flourishes in partial shade or shade
Care: Keep evenly damp; feed every one to two weeks until August; if shaping in late summer or spring, do not use shears but trim shoots individually; bring indoors late, tolerates some frost; winter over in a bright place, if necessary in a dark one, at 32–43 °F (0–6 °C), water sparingly, can be brought back outdoors in mid-April
Propagation: From cuttings, but it is time-consuming
Design: Often trained into pyramidal or spherical shapes, but is also attractive if left unshaped
Tip: Once dried, the bay leaves can be used for culinary purposes.

Height:
*1–3 ft
(0.3–0.9 m)*
Bloom Time:
*June–
August*

*evergreen
semishrub*

Lavandula angustifolia

Lavender

Family: Mint (Lamiaceae)
Origin: Mediterranean region
Description: Blue-violet, white, or pink labiate flowers in slender ears, aromatically scented; growth: erect, bushy; narrow, linear, silvery-gray leaves with an aromatic scent
Location: If possible, full sun; warm
Care: Water only in prolonged dry weather; trim shoots by 1/3 in spring; feed only every couple of years after cutting back; loves nonacid soil; winter over outdoors with winter protection, in heavy frosts put indoors in a bright, cool place
Propagation: From tip cuttings in summer, the pure species also from seed in spring
Design: Even in a pot, lavender is a suitable, attractive partner for roses; it also fits in well with Mediterranean arrangements, groups of herbs, and combinations of scented plants.

Height:
*1–6 ft
(0.3–2 m)*
Bloom Time:
May–June

*evergreen
tree/
shrub*

Leptospermum scoparium

New Zealand Tea Tree

Family: Myrtle (Myrtaceae)
Origin: Australia, New Zealand
Description: Numerous small flowers in pink, red, or white, single or double; densely branching growth; needle-like leaves, depending on cultivar green, blue-green, or bronze, exuding aromatic scent when rubbed
Location: Sunny; warm
Care: Water generously in summer, but avoid standing water, dryness causes the leaves to drop; until August, feed every two weeks; sensitive to lime, so use only soft water, rhododendron planting medium, and food; thin and cut back lightly right after the bloom; winter over in a bright place at 41–50 °F (5–10 °C)
Propagation: From tip cuttings in summer or from seed in spring
Design: Pretty with eucalyptus and bottlebrush, also native to Australia; also trained as standard

Height:
1.5–4 ft
(0.5–1.2 m)
Bloom Time:
June–
August

bulbous
plant

Lilium Hybrids and Species

Lily

Family: Lily (Liliaceae)
Origin: Asia, America, Europe
Description: Flowers in shades of yellow, orange, pink, and red or in white, shaped like funnels, trumpets, or bowls; growth: stiffly erect, with thick stalks
Location: Sunny; fire lily and Turk's cap lily also in partial shade
Care: Keep well dampened, but avoid standing water at all costs; provide slow-release fertilizer in spring; cut off faded flowers, stake; in late fall cut withered stems back hard, and winter over in a dark place at 32–41 °F (0–5 °C), don't allow to dry out completely, put in a bright place when new growth begins
Propagation: From seed or by removing and planting bulb scales
Design: Very pretty in blue or white pots, lovely with blue- or white-flowering companions
Tip: Plant bulbs in fall or spring, 8 in. (20 cm) deep and 6–8 in. (15–20 cm) apart, good drainage necessary

Height:
*up to 13 ft
(4 m)*
Bloom Time:
*May–June
or June–
August*

*usually
deciduous
climbing
shrubs*

Lonicera Species

Honeysuckle

Family: Honeysuckle (Caprifoliaceae)
Origin: Europe, North America, East Asia
Description: Tubular flowers, depending on cultivar yellowish white to red, intensely scented in the evening; from August on, red or black poisonous berries; twining plants with ovate leaves
Location: Partial shade to shade
Care: Keep damp; use slow-release fertilizer in spring; thin out occasionally; can be cut back; winter over outdoors, protect root area in hard frost
Propagation: From cuttings
Design: Very versatile, usable to cover walls, create visual screen, adorn fences and pergolas
Species/Cultivars: Bloom in May–June: Italian honeysuckle (*L. caprofolium*) and common honeysuckle (*L. periclymenum*), both with yellowish-white flowers, with a hint of red; bloom in June–August: *L.* x *heckrottii*, *L.* x *brownii* (both orange to red), redgold honeysuckle (*L.* x *tellmanniana*), yellow, and Henry honeysuckle (*L. henryi*), yellowish red

Height:
*1.5–8 ft
(1.5–2.5 m)*
Bloom Time:
*July–
October*

*deciduous
shrub*

Lycianthes rantonnetii

Paraguay Nightshade

Other Names: Blue potato bush; previously botanically classi-
fied as *Solanum*
Family: Nightshade (Solanaceae)
Origin: Argentina, Paraguay
Description: Flowers blue-violet with yellow eye; growth:
dense and bushy, with some overhanging shoots, also climb-
ing, quite fast-growing and aggressive
Location: Sunny to partial shade
Care: In summer, permeate with water; feed weekly until
August; prune young plants often to promote bushy growth;
winter over in a dark place at 39–50 °F (4–10 °C), cut back by
half before bringing indoors, water very sparingly in winter
quarters
Propagation: From semiripe cuttings in summer
Design: Especially handsome as a standard with underplanting, for example, with red hanging verbena or Dahlberg daisies
Tip: The climbing *Solanum jasminoides* resembles a white-
blooming version of Paraguay nightshade.

Height:
*6–16 ft
(2–5 m)*
Bloom Time:
*June–
August*

*semiever-
green
climbing
shrub*

Mandevilla laxa
Chilean Jasmine

Family: Dogbane (Apocynaceae)
Origin: Bolivia, Argentina
Description: Trumpet-shaped flowers, white, scented, in racemes; twining plant with long, lignifying shoots; ovate, glossy dark-green leaves (usually shedding in fall in cooler climates)
Location: Sunny
Care: Keep well dampened; feed weekly until August; train on stakes or climbing frame; tolerates some frost, bring indoors late after trimming moderately (then thin out in spring) or cut back to 8 in. (20 cm); winter over in a dark place at 39–46 °F (4–8 °C), keep almost dry after leaves fall
Propagation: From seed or semiripe cuttings
Design: Unusual flowering plant and also a decorative foliage plant; when trained to grow up a trellis, makes an attractive backdrop for other bloomers
Tip: The shoots contain a toxic milky juice, so be careful when cutting!

Height:
*20–60 in.
(0.5–1.5 m)*
Bloom Time:
*June–
October*

*evergreen
shrub*

Myrtus communis
True Myrtle

Family: Myrtle (Myrtaceae)
Origin: Mediterranean region
Description: Flowers white, small, star-shaped, scented; sometimes blue-black berries (nontoxic) appear; growth: dense, bushy, branching, and quite compact; small, lanceolate, dark-green leaves (contain toxins), exuding an aromatic scent when rubbed
Location: Prefers full sun
Care: Keep evenly damp, avoid drying out of root-ball and standing water at all costs, use soft water if possible; feed weekly until August (rhododendron food); pot in slightly acid soil; pinch tips of young plants often; winter over in a bright place at 41–50 °F (5–10 °C)
Propagation: From tip cuttings in late summer or early spring
Design: Fits well into Mediterranean arrangements, for example, with oleander, small citrus trees, and rosemary; can also be shaped or trained as a standard

Height:
*5–8 ft
(1.5–2.5 m)*
Bloom Time:
*June–
October*

*evergreen
shrub*

Nerium oleander

Oleander

Family: Dogbane (Apocynaceae)
Origin: Mediterranean region
Description: Flowers pink, white, red, yellow, apricot, single or double, in umbel-like inflorescences, some scented; growth: loosely branching; lanceolate, leathery leaves
Location: Prefers full sun, but also tolerates some shade; protect from rain, especially double cultivars
Care: Water generously, fill pot saucer with water; feed weekly until August; prune with restraint, since flowers are already set the previous year, occasionally remove bare and overly long shoots in fall or spring; best to winter over in a bright place at 39–46 °F (4–8 °C), almost dry, if necessary also in a dark place, or warmer (up to 59 °F (15 °C)), then if possible in a bright place and with more frequent watering
Propagation: From cuttings in summer
Design: Terra-cotta tubs accentuate the Mediterranean flair; pretty with bougainvillea and fig
Tip: Be careful, all parts of the plant are highly toxic!

Height:
5–6.5 ft
(1.5–2 m)
Bloom Time:
July–August

evergreen shrub

Olea europaea

Olive Tree

Family: Olive (Oleaceae)
Origin: Mediterranean region
Description: Flowers yellowish white, in racemes, inconspicuous, lightly scented; growth: often leggy at first, bushier with time and frequent pruning; narrow lanceolate, blue-green leaves, with silvery hair beneath
Location: Prefers full sun
Care: Keep moderately damp; feed every two weeks until August; light cutting back every one to two years; winter over in a light or dark place at 36–50 °F (2–10 °C), if in dark place leaves will fall, then keep almost dry; older plants tolerate some frost, bring indoors late and take back out in April
Propagation: From cuttings in summer or from seed in spring
Design: Attractive in groups with blooming Mediterranean container plants and small citrus trees
Tip: Self-fertilizing, grafted specimens bear fruit, though in colder climates it does not always ripen

Height:
*3–6.5 ft
(1–2 m)*
Bloom Time:
*April–
October*

*evergreen
climbing
shrub*

Passiflora caerulea

Blue Passionflower

Family: Passionflower (Passifloraceae)
Origin: South America
Description: Large flowers with white sepals and petals below a corona with violet-white-blue circular zones, cultivars with color variants, up to 4 in. (10 cm) across; twining shoots with lobed leaves
Location: Sunny; protected
Care: Water abundantly in summer, but avoid standing water; feed weekly until August; provide support for shoots (stakes, rings in the pot, or train it up a frame); before moving it indoors, trim long shoots, winter over in a bright place at 36–50 °F (2–10 °C), keep almost dry
Propagation: From cuttings in spring or from seed
Design: The unusual, large-flowered twining plant is most effective when used alone.
Species/Cultivars: Also able to spend the summer outdoors is *P. edulis,* whose fruit (passion fruit) ripens in warm late summers, though it does so more readily in a conservatory.

P

Height:
3–10 ft
(1–3 m)
Bloom Time:
not
applicable

evergreen
rosette-tree

Phoenix canariensis

Canary Island Date Palm

Family: Palm (Arecaceae)
Origin: Canary Islands
Description: Flowers yellow, but very rare in container culture; growth: spreading and fast-growing, with stout trunk; large, feathery palm fronds with narrow leaf segments
Location: Sunny, likes full sun
Care: Needs plenty of water, but avoid both standing water and root-ball dryness (causes brown tips) at all costs; feed every two to three weeks until August; cut off dried-out fronds; winter over in a bright place at 41–50 °F (5–10 °C), keep almost dry; when bringing outdoors in May, first put in shade, move into full sun only after about two weeks
Propagation: From seed in spring
Design: Decorative palm, eye-catching even when used alone; if there is enough room, it is gorgeous in a little group with angel's trumpet, pink rockrose, or bougainvillea; can also be underplanted with small summer flowers

Height:
*3–6.5 ft
(1–2 m)*
Bloom Time:
*August–
September*

*evergreen
herbaceous
perennial*

Phormium tenax

New Zealand Flax

Family: Phormiaceae
Origin: New Zealand
Description: Reddish panicles on a long shaft, appearing only when specimens are about six years old; clump-like growth; long, sword-shaped leaves, at first stiffly erect, then pendent over time, depending on cultivar striped with green, bronze, or multiple colors (reddish, yellow, and/or white)
Location: Full sun to shade
Care: Water copiously in a sunny place, otherwise moderately, no standing water; feed weekly until August; tolerates light frost, bring indoors late; winter over in a light or dark place at 39–50 °F (4–10 °C), water sparingly, remove dried leaves from time to time
Propagation: By division in spring
Design: Very appealing in rectangular terra-cotta pots, older plants especially impressive in barrel halves; can be under-planted with summer flowers and hanging plants such as ivy

Height:
*1–3 ft
(0.3–1 m)*
Bloom Time:
*not
applicable*

*evergreen
conifer*

Picea Species in Cultivars
Dwarf Spruce

Family: Pine (Pinaceae)
Origin: Europe, North America
Description: Usually spherical to rounded growth habit; needles regularly arranged, often very densely needled
Location: Best in light shade, low tolerance of full sun and dry air
Care: Keep evenly damp; provide slow-release fertilizer in spring, add food (conifer fertilizer) in summer for larger specimens; winter over outdoors, protect root area in heavy frost
Propagation: Not applicable, as it is grafted
Design: Especially suitable for long-term plantings in troughs, small specimens also good in winter boxes
Species/Cultivars: Selection: *P. abies* 'Little Gem' (hemispheric, green-needled), *P. glauca* 'Echiniformis' (shallow sphere, blue-green), 'Conica' (spherical, blue-green), *P. omorika* 'Nana' (spherical, green), *P. pungens* 'Glauca Globosa' (shallow sphere, silvery blue)

Height:
*1–2 ft
(0.3–0.6 m)*
Bloom Time:
*not
applicable*

*evergreen
conifer*

Pinus Species in Cultivars
Dwarf Pine

Family: Pine (Pinaceae)
Origin: Northern temperate zone
Description: Usually compact, rounded growth; in some cases, very long needles
Location: Sunny, also full sun
Care: Keep evenly and slightly damp; provide slow-release fertilizer in spring, in summer feed large specimens again (conifer food); winter over outdoors, protect root area in heavy frost
Propagation: Not applicable, as it is often grafted
Design: Dwarf pines fit well into Mediterranean arrangements or with rock-garden plants in containers
Species/Cultivars: Selection: *P. densiflora* 'Kobold' (spherical, green-needled), 'Globosa' (shallow sphere, green); *P. mugo* 'Gnom,' 'Humpy,' 'Mops,' 'Mini Mops,' 'Pumilio' (all hemispheric to spherical, green), 'Ophir' (broad and bushy, green); *P. nigra* 'Spielberg' (rounded to broad and spherical, green); *P. pumila* 'Glauca' (broad and bushy, blue-green)

Height:
*1.5–6 ft
(0.5–2 m)*
Bloom Time:
*June–
October*

*evergreen
shrub*

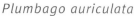

Plumbago auriculata

Cape Plumbago

Family: Leadwort (Plumbaginaceae)
Origin: South Africa
Description: Flowers light blue, light violet, white, small, in umbel-like inflorescences; growth: loose, bushy, with over-hanging, somewhat brittle shoots
Location: Prefers full sun; protected from wind and rain if possible
Care: Needs abundant water in summer, but avoid standing water; feed every two weeks until August; remove faded flowers; stake shoots if needed; cut back (if necessary) in fall, in spring occasionally thin out overmature branches; winter over in a bright place at 39–46 °F (4–8 °C), in a dark place if necessary, but then cut back heavily before bringing indoors, put in a brighter, warmer place in March
Propagation: From semiripe tip cuttings in summer
Design: Especially pretty as a standard; as a young plant can also be used for mixed balcony boxes and hanging planters

Height:
*5–10 ft
(1.5–3 m)*
Bloom Time:
*July–
October*

*evergreen
climbing
shrub*

Podranea ricasoliana

Port St. John's Creeper

Family: Trumpet creeper (Bignoniaceae)
Origin: South Africa
Description: Rose-colored flowers with red veining, broad, funnel-shaped, and large, up to 2 in. (5 cm) across, in bunches; climbing with long, lignifying shoots, fast-growing, also bushy or trainable as a standard; pinnate leaves
Location: Sunny; protected from rain
Care: Water generously in summer; feed weekly until August (low-nitrogen food, otherwise threat of very heavy shoot growth with reduced bloom); train with supports or climbing frame; frequent cutting back promotes bushy growth; winter over in a bright place at 41–59 °F (5–15 °C), if need be keep in a dark place, cool and almost dry, then all the leaves will fall
Propagation: From tip cuttings in February
Design: As a fast-growing climber on a trellis, it soon creates a wonderful visual screen, or it can be used as a wonderful wall decoration; however, it is also lovely as a shrub (prune frequently).

Height:
*3–5 ft
(1–1.5 m)*
Bloom Time:
May–June

*evergreen
shrub*

Prunus laurocerasus

Cherry Laurel

Other Name: English laurel
Family: Rose (Rosaceae)
Origin: Southeastern Europe, Near East
Description: White, small flowers in erect, long racemes, heavily scented; pea-sized black fruit (toxic!); growth: depending on cultivar, erect and spherical or prostrate; elongated, glossy, dark-green leaves
Location: Preferably in partial shade, not in blazing sun, also in shade
Care: Water moderately, more often if in sunny place; feed every four weeks until August; tolerates cutting; winter over outdoors, protection essential, best to wrap up entire plant if frost is heavy
Propagation: From cuttings in fall
Design: Ornamental foliage plant for partial shade and shade; pretty alone, also with blooming plants such as fuchsia or hydrangea
Tip: All parts of the plant are quite poisonous!

Height:
*1.5–6.5 ft
(0.5–2 m)*
Bloom Time:
*June–
September*

*evergreen
shrub/
tree*

Punica granatum

Pomegranate Tree

Family: Pomegranate (Punicaceae)
Origin: Near East
Description: Flowers brilliant red, white, or yellow-orange, funnel-shaped; sometimes bears fruit even in this country, but the rounded pomegranates usually ripen only in a conservatory; usually bushy growth or trained as a standard; narrow, ovate, glossy green leaves
Location: Sunny, also full sun
Care: Water generously only until roughly late July and feed every two weeks; then keep drier; occasionally thin out older specimens in spring; older specimens also tolerate some frost; winter over in a bright or dark place at 36–46 °F (2–8 °C), keep almost dry
Propagation: From stalk cuttings in spring or tip cuttings in summer, also from seed
Design: This plant, which has become naturalized in the Mediterranean region, enriches any Mediterranean arrangement; group for example, with true myrtle, oleander, and small citrus trees.

R

Height:
20–40 in.
(0.5–1 m)
Bloom Time:
April–May/
June

evergreen
shrub

Rhododendron Species and Hybrids

Rhododendron, Azalea

Family: Heather (Ericaceae)
Origin: East Asia
Description: Flowers red, pink, lilac, white, or yellow, in racemes; growth: broad, bushy; dark-green, glossy leaves
Location: Preferably in partial shade, absolutely no blazing midday sun
Care: Not lime-tolerant, use only soft water or rainwater, rhododendron soil and food; water generously in spring/summer, the rest of the year keep only slightly damp; from April to June feed every three to four weeks; break off faded inflorescences; winter over outdoors with winter protection
Propagation: Not applicable in container culture
Design: Pretty in barrel halves or terra-cotta tubs
Species/Cultivars: Especially good for containers:
R. yakushima, forrestii, and *repens* hybrids; small 'Diamant' azaleas also for balcony boxes

Height:
*8–16 in.
(0.2–0.4 m)*
Bloom Time:
*June–
October*

*deciduous
dwarf shrub*

Rosa Hybrids
Small Rose

Family: Rose (Rosaceae)
Origin: Cultivated forms
Description: Flowers in all colors except blue, usually semi-double or double, rarely scented; growth: bushy, with thorny shoots
Location: Sunny
Care: Keep moderately damp; feed every two weeks until late July; cut off faded inflorescences together with the leaf pair below; cut back in spring; winter over in a bright, frost-free place, if necessary in a dark place or outdoors with good protection
Propagation: Not applicable, as it usually is grafted
Design: Dwarf roses are enchanting in small pots or in groups in large boxes, planted 10 in. (25 cm) apart
Tip: In addition to the dwarf or miniature roses, medium- to long-stemmed, trailing cultivars are available, and they are good in hanging planters.

Height:
20–60 in.
(0.5–1.5 m)
Bloom Time:
June–
October

deciduous
shrub

Rosa Hybrids

Rose, Taller Cultivars

Family: Rose (Rosaceae)
Origin: Cultivated forms
Description: Flowers in all colors except blue, usually semi-double or double, some intensely scented; growth: bushy, erect, or overhanging; thorny shoots
Location: Sunny
Care: As for dwarf roses, but best to apply slow-release fertilizer in spring; winter over outdoors with good protection (also cover graft site, wrap up standards before spells of frost); in locations with harsh weather, better in a frost-free, bright place, if necessary in a dark one
Propagation: Not applicable, as it usually is grafted
Design: The classic, attractive partner for roses, even in containers, is lavender (in a separate, neighboring pot). Other pretty companions are, for example, daisy bushes or marguerite daisies.
Species/Cultivars: Roses that stay low, such as bedding, shrubby, and groundcover roses, as well as roses trained as standards, are suitable for planting alone in containers.

Height:
*3–8 ft
(1–2.5 m)*
Bloom Time:
*June–
October*

*evergreen
shrub*

Senna corymbosa

Argentine Senna

Other Name: Often still listed under the previous botanical
name, *Cassia corymbosa*
Family: Carob (Caesalpiniaceae)
Origin: South America
Description: Very numerous yellow flowers, in conservatory
appearing almost year-round; growth: erect, branching
Location: Full sun, if possible; warm and protected from wind
Care: Keep well dampened; feed weekly until August; deadhead; cut back in spring; tolerates light frost, don't bring
indoors too early; winter over in a bright place at 36–41 °F
(2–5 °C), if need be also in a dark one, after cutting back
before taking it indoors, and then the leaves will be shed (in
this case, keep almost dry)
Propagation: From softwood cuttings
Design: Easy to train as a standard
Species/Cultivars: In popcorn senna, *S. didymobotrya*, which
needs similar care, the yellow flowers are erect on the shoot
tips, resembling candles.

Height:
*5–10 ft
(1.5–3 m)*
Bloom Time:
*May–
October*

*deciduous
shrub*

Sesbania tripetii
Scarlet Wisteria

Other Name: Botanically, also known as *S. punicae*
Family: Legume (Fabaceae)
Origin: South America
Description: Orange-red papilionaceous flowers in hanging panicles; growth: loose, bushy; pretty, regularly pinnate leaves
Location: Sunny, also full sun; needs a place as warm and protected from rain as possible
Care: Keep evenly damp, leaves and blooms will drop if soil dries out; feed every two weeks until late July; break off fructifications regularly; prune young plants often to promote bushy growth; even older specimens can be cut back hard in spring; winter over in a dark place at 39–46 °F (4–8 °C), keep almost dark
Propagation: From semilignified tip cuttings in summer
Design: As a bush or a standard, an attractive plant that can be combined with many exotic and Mediterranean plants

Height:
1.5–3 ft.
(0.5–1 m)
Bloom Time:
April–May

*evergreen
dwarf shrub*

Skimmia japonica

Japanese Skimmia

Family: Citrus (Rutaceae)
Origin: East Asia
Description: Small flowers, whitish pink, in dense panicles; in the pure species and some cultivars, numerous, long-lasting, scarlet-red globular fruits, starting in fall (inedible); growth: broad, bushy; decorative, laurel-like leaves
Location: Partial shade to shade
Care: From early summer on, water abundantly; feed every four weeks until mid-August; cut off only shoots that are in the way; winter over outdoors, protect root area from hard frosts
Propagation: From cuttings in fall
Design: As a young plant, pretty in winter boxes, otherwise suitable for permanent plantings, for example, with dwarf conifers, small rhododendrons, and Scotch heather
Species/Cultivars: Some cultivars, such as the frequently available 'Rubella,' bear no fruit and are grown for their luxuriant bloom.

Height:
3–6 ft
(1–2 m)
Bloom Time:
February–
August

evergreen
herbaceous
perennial

Strelitzia reginae
Bird of Paradise Flower

Other Name: Strelitzia, crane flower
Family: Strelitzia (Strelitziaceae)
Origin: South Africa
Description: Flowers yellow-orange with sky blue, in reddish green bracts, inflorescence on long scape, reminiscent of bird's head; clump-like growth; long-stemmed, large, narrow oval leaves
Location: Sunny; protected from wind
Care: Keep moderately damp but not wet; feed every two weeks until August; occasionally thin out the oldest leaves; winter over in a bright place at 46–54 °F (8–12 °C), with enough light also warmer, the cooler it is, the drier you should keep it
Propagation: By division of older plants in spring or from seed; the latter is time-consuming, however
Design: Accompanied by canna and palms, it lends a luxurious, exotic note. Bird of paradise flower is also very attractive alone, however.
Tip: Lasts well as a cut flower for striking arrangements

Height:
8–32 in.
(0.2–0.8 m)
Bloom Time:
not
applicable

evergreen
conifer

Thuja Species in Cultivars
Arborvitae

Other Name: Cedar
Family: Cypress (Cupressaceae)
Origin: North America, East Asia
Description: Usually spherical to conical growth; flat, closely placed scale-like leaves, in cultivars sometimes appealingly yellow, in winter brownish
Location: Sunny to partial shade; ideally in a place somewhat protected from rain
Care: Keep evenly damp; use slow-release fertilizer in spring, add more in June/July for larger specimens (conifer food); winter over outdoors, protect root area in hard frost
Propagation: From cuttings
Design: Pretty for long-term plantings; yellow-needled cultivars brighten winter plantings
Species/Cultivars: Selection: *T. occidentalis* 'Danica' (spherical, green-needled), 'Recurva Nana' (broad and spherical, green), 'Rheingold' (conical, yellow), 'Sunkist' (conical, yellow), 'Tiny Tim' (spherical, green)

Height:
*3–6.5 ft
(1–2 m)*
Bloom Time:
*late July–
October*

*evergreen
shrub*

Tibouchina urvilleana

Princess Flower

Family: Melastomataceae
Origin: Brazil
Description: Large, bowl-shaped flowers in bright violet, in a conservatory blooming until spring; growth habit: broad, somewhat leggy, with long shoots; large, broad, ovate, velvety looking leaves
Location: Sunny, also light shade, no blazing midday sun if at all possible
Care: Keep evenly damp but not wet, use soft, low-lime water if possible; feed every two weeks until August; regularly pinch back shoot tips—especially in young plants—to promote bushy growth; winter over in a bright place at 41–50 °F (5–10 °C)
Propagation: From tip cuttings in spring or summer
Design: If possible, place in front of white wall to show off the violet flowers; also unusual as a standard; pretty as underplanting with creeping zinnia or Dahlberg daisies

Height:
*5–13 ft
(1.5–4 m)*
Bloom Time:
June–July

*evergreen
rosette-tree*

Trachycarpus fortunei
Chusan Palm

Family: Palm (Arecaceae)
Origin: East Asia
Description: Greenish or yellow panicles, only on older plants; grows very slowly, but becomes outspreading over time; large, shiny green fronds, subdivided like fans, over 1.5 ft (50 cm) long
Location: Young chusan palms best in partial shade, older specimens in sun
Care: Keep moderately damp; feed every three to four weeks until August; cut out brown fronds; older plants tolerate up to 14 °F (−10 °C), but with good protection can be wintered over outdoors in regions with mild winters; otherwise, in a dark place at 32–46 °F (0–8 °C), or in a bright place as an indoor plant; water sparingly, never get heart wet; after moving outdoors from mid-April on, first put in shade
Propagation: From seed
Design: Very decorative palm, attractive background for exotic bloomers

Height:
*55–70 in.
(1.4–1.8 m)*
Bloom Time:
*September–
April*

*evergreen
shrub*

Viburnum tinus

Laurustinus

Other Name: Viburnum
Family: Honeysuckle (Caprifoliaceae)
Origin: Mediterranean region
Description: Flowers white or delicate pink, numerous in flat panicles, scented; growth: bushy, branching; narrow ovate, glossy dark-green, leathery leaves
Location: Sunny, but no blazing midday sun, or partial shade (not too dark)
Care: Keep evenly damp; feed weekly until late July; prune young plants frequently, tolerates cutting well; if necessary, best to cut in spring after the bloom; tolerates some frost; winter over in a bright place at 32–46 °F (0–8 °C), water moderately
Propagation: From softwood cuttings in summer
Design: Depending on location and development, the main bloom comes in fall or spring; in a conservatory or a bright hallway, laurustinus even flowers in winter.

Height:
*5–10 ft
(1.5–3 m)*
Bloom Time:
*not
applicable*

*evergreen
rosette-tree*

Washingtonia Species

Washingtonia

Family: Palm (Arecaceae)
Origin: Southern North America, Mexico
Description: Flowers white or light pink, rare in container culture; broad, outspread growth with thick trunk; rounded fronds subdivided like fans, in *W. filifera* with dangling, light filaments; thorny pedicels
Location: Sunny, but don't put young palms in full sun in the first few years
Care: Keep damp in summer, but don't soak; feed low doses every two weeks until August; winter over in a bright place at 41–46 °F (5–8 °C), if necessary in a dark place at 41 °F (5 °C); after moving outdoors, put in light shade at first; *W. filifera* tolerates some frost
Propagation: From seed
Design: Imposing palm for using alone
Species/Cultivars: *W. robusta,* despite its name, is less robust and less tolerant of cold than *W. filifera.*

Height:
3–6.5 ft
(1–2 m)
Bloom Time:
July–
September

evergreen
rosette-tree

Yucca aloifolia

Spanish Bayonet

Family: Agave (Agavaceae)
Origin: South America
Description: White bell flowers in panicles on long shaft, only on older specimens and rare in container culture; long, sword-shaped leaves on slender stalk; be careful, the thorny tips are dangerous!
Location: Sunny, also full sun
Care: Keep moderately damp; feed every four weeks until August; cut off brown leaves; overly large specimens put forth again after the stems are shortened (sawed off); winter over in a bright place at 41–50 °F (5–10 °C), keep almost dry
Propagation: From tip or stem cuttings in summer; put pots in shade
Design: Can be combined with many other container plants, pretty next to plumbago or lantana
Species/Cultivars: The giant or spineless yucca, *Y. elephantipes,* has somewhat softer leaves, branches heavily over the years, and is a more dependable bloomer in container culture when it is older.

Tasty Choices
from A to Z

Harvest your own crop—fresh from the balcony box or pot right to your table. That's already a plus. In addition, many kinds of herbs, vegetables, and fruits have beautiful flowers and leaves. And the fruit they bear is a special delight to the eye, as well as a promise of pleasure to the palate.

Height:
*up to 10 ft
(3 m)*
**Harvest
Time:**
*October–
November*

*evergreen
climbing
shrub*

Actinidia deliciosa

Kiwi

Family: Kiwi fruit (Actinidiaceae)
Origin: East Asia
Description: Twining plant; white flowers in June–July, usually female and male flowers on different plants (dioecious); brown berries
Location: Bright place, but not full sun; protected from wind, warm, best to train up the house wall
Cultivation: With dioecious cultivars, one female and one male specimen are needed for formation of fruit
Care: Train on sturdy climbing frame; keep good and damp; supply slow-release fertilizer in spring, add more in June and early August; in summer, shorten lateral shoots to four to six leaves above the fruits; winter over outdoors with good protection
Harvesting: Starting in late October, when the fruits give slightly to pressure
Species/Cultivars: Reliable cultivars are 'Hayward,' 'Weiki' (very frost-hardy), and 'Jenny' (monoecious, self-fertilizing).

Height:
8–12 in.
(20–30 cm)
Harvest Time:
continuously until fall

perennial herb

Allium schoenoprasum var. schoenoprasum

Chives

Family: Onion (Alliaceae)
Origin: Northern temperate zone
Description: Dense clumps of tubular, thin leaves; from June–August/September, light violet umbels on thick shafts
Location: Sun to partial shade
Cultivation: Grow in March/April at 64–68 °F (18–20 °C); plant seedlings in bunches (of 10–20), 8 in. (20 cm) apart, in planters; starting in April, put them outdoors, cover in case of frost; can easily be combined with lettuce or with other herbs
Care: Keep evenly damp, but avoid standing water; feed every two weeks until August; breaking off the inflorescences promotes leaf development but is not essential; winter over in a bright, cool place; every two to three years, divide in fall or spring and replant
Harvesting: About six weeks after sowing, cut off leaves 3/4 in. (2 cm) above the substrate surface, and then let new growth develop again

Height:
*12–20 in.
(30–50 cm)*
**Harvest
Time:**
*July–
October*

*greens
grown
as an
annual*

B

Beta vulgaris ssp. cicla

Swiss Chard

Family: Goosefoot (Chenopodiaceae)
Origin: Near East, Mediterranean region
Description: Erect, wrinkled leaves; stalks white, yellow, or bright red
Location: Sun to partial shade
Cultivation: From late April–June, sow 2–4 in. (5–10 cm) apart in large pots or boxes; thin out young plants to a distance of 8 in. (20 cm; smaller spinach beet) or 12 in. (30 cm; chard), removing the weakest plants altogether
Care: Always keep well dampened; feed with low-nitrogen fertilizer every four weeks
Harvesting: First harvest spinach beet about 8 weeks, chard about 12 weeks after sowing, then harvest continually; for chard, leave inner leaves ("heart") alone
Species/Cultivars: Reliable cultivar: 'Lukullus,' both spinach beet and chard; decorative red-stalked cultivars: 'Vulkan,' 'Feurio,' 'Rhubarb Chard,' 'Bright Lights' with stalks of various colors (in shades of red and gold)

Height:
*20–24 in.
(50–60 cm)*
**Harvest
Time:**
*July–
September*

*annual
vegetable*

Cucurbita pepo
Zucchini

Family: Gourd (Cucurbitaceae)
Origin: Central America, southern North America
Description: Spreading growth, some cultivars also climb; large, light-green or silver-flecked leaves covered with coarse hairs; golden-yellow to orange funnel-shaped flowers, blooming from June to August; cylindrical or club-shaped fruit, depending on cultivar, green, yellow, white, or striped
Location: Sunny, also light shade; warm, protected
Cultivation: In late April, sow two seeds per pot, with germination temperature of about 68 °F (20 °C); after they sprout, remove weaker plants; plant in broad containers, place outdoors after mid-May; usually one or two plants suffice
Care: Keep well dampened, but don't pour water into the flowers; feed weekly
Harvesting: Starting about six weeks after planting, harvest ripe fruit continually; fruit tastes best when 6–8 in. (15–20 cm) long; don't tear or twist off stems, but cut off with a sharp knife

Height:
*4–8 in.
(10–20 cm)*
**Harvest
Time:**
*May–
October*

E

Eruca sativa

Arugula

Other Name: Rocket
Family: Mustard or cabbage (Brassicaeae)
Origin: Mediterranean region
Description: Forms rosette of lobed or deeply notched leaves with strongly spicy, nutty taste
Location: Sunny to partial shade
Cultivation: From April–September, sow directly in planter, in rows 6–8 in. (15–20 cm) apart, or broadcast; cover seed only lightly with soil
Care: Keep evenly damp, avoid standing water; one to two weeks after sowing, feed sparingly and/or with low-nitrogen fertilizer
Harvesting: Three to five weeks after sowing; if you pick individual leaves, you can harvest several times; preferably harvest leaves while young and tender, as older leaves quickly develop a strong taste, especially in summer
Species/Cultivars: The cultivar 'Runway' is especially fast-growing and has finely pinnate leaves.

Height:
*8–12 in.
(20–30 cm)*
**Harvest
Time:** *June–
October*

*herbaceous
perennial*

Fragaria Species
Strawberry

Family: Rose (Rosaceae)
Origin: Europe, America
Description: Bushy growth with above-ground runners
(except with ever-flowering woodland strawberries); white or
pink flowers; bloom time: May–September; red fruit
Location: Sunny; for ever-flowering woodland strawberries,
also partial shade
Cultivation: Plant in July–September or spring; singly in large
containers or 12 in. (30 cm) apart
Care: Keep evenly damp; use slow-release fertilizer in spring;
remove withered leaves in fall; winter over outdoors with protection
Harvesting: Separate fruit along with the calyx
Species/Cultivars: Suitable for containers are ever-flowering
woodland strawberries, with small fruit (harvest in June/July);
large-fruit garden strawberries, which bear repeatedly (harvest
in June–October); as well as cultivated kinds with long shoots
or runners, such as hanging strawberries long, also for hanging planters) and climbing strawberries.

Height:
*8–12 in.
(20–30 cm)*
**Harvest
Time:**
*from
April/May*

*salad plant
grown as an
annual*

Lactuca sativa var. crispa

Leaf Lettuce, Curly Lettuce

Family: Aster, daisy, or sunflower (Asteraceae)
Origin: Presumably from northeastern Africa or western Asia
Description: Loose to dense rosettes of smooth or curly all over or just along the edges, green, reddish, or brownish leaves
Location: Preferably sunny, also partial shade
Cultivation: Can be sown from seed, starting in February, at 50–59 °F (10–15 °C); sow cutting lettuce in two rows or broadcast directly in box; raise leaf lettuce and plant 8–10 in. (20–25 cm) apart; put outdoors, with protection, from April on; second sowing of curly lettuce until April, of leaf lettuce until July
Care: Keep evenly damp; feed low dose after every cutting
Harvesting: Starting four to six weeks after sowing; for cutting lettuce, cut the entire plant off the stalk, for leaf lettuce harvest the outer leaves continually
Species/Cultivars: A reliable balcony cultivar is 'Grand Rapids,' a leaf lettuce.

Height:
*8–12 in.
(20–30 cm)*
**Harvest
Time:**
*March–
October*

annual herb

Lepidium sativum

Garden Cress

Family: Mustard or cabbage (Brassicaceae)
Origin: Mediterranean region, southwestern Asia
Description: Delicate shoots with small, round leaves, fast-growing; starting in July, white to reddish flowers
Location: Sunny or partial shade, even grows in shade with sufficient warmth
Cultivation: From March to September, sow directly in boxes or bowls, repeat sowings every two weeks; broadcast seed, press gently, and cover lightly with soil; no thinning out of seedlings required
Care: Keep evenly damp; no feeding necessary
Harvesting: About ten days after sowing, the young shoots can be cut off directly above the surface of the soil, once they are about 2.5 in. (6 cm) high
Tip: Garden cress is an unproblematic partner for combination in balcony boxes and can quickly be sown in a vacant spot next to tomatoes or between radishes or other herbs.

Height:
10–47 in.
(25–120
cm)
**Harvest
Time:**
*July–
October*

*annual
plant
with edible
fruit*

L

Lycopersicon esculentum

Bush and Cocktail Tomatoes

Family: Nightshade (Solanaceae)
Origin: South America
Description: Growth habit depends on cultivar; from May on, yellow flowers; usually rounded red or yellow fruit
Location: Sunny; warm and protected
Cultivation: Sow seeds starting in late February/March, at 68 °F (20 °C); prick out singly into 4-in. (10–cm) pots, grow at a temperature of 64 °F (18 °C); plant at least 14 in. (35 cm) apart, putting high cultivars in individual pots; put outdoors starting in mid-May
Care: Keep well dampened; feed weekly; remove withered leaves at the base; tie cocktail tomato plants to stakes; no pruning needed
Harvesting: From July on, pick fully ripe fruit
Species/Cultivars: Bush tomatoes: short plants, medium-sized fruit; cocktail or cherry tomatoes: high plants, small, often sweetish fruit; hanging tomatoes: medium-sized to small fruit; staked tomatoes (→ page 214)
Tip: Green parts of the plants contain toxins.

Height:
3–5 ft
(1–1.5 m)
Harvest Time:
July–October

annual plant with edible fruit

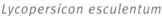

Lycopersicon esculentum

Staked Tomato

Family: Nightshade (Solanaceae)
Origin: South America
Description: High, with little branching; from May on, yellow flowers; usually large red or yellow fruit, in beefsteak tomatoes especially large and furrowed
Location: Sunny; warm and protected
Cultivation: As for bush and cocktail tomatoes; in addition, regularly break off axillary shoots of young plants; tie plants to stakes; after formation of the fifth inflorescence or arrangement of fruits, clip the tip of the main stem
Harvesting: Pick fully ripe fruit, starting in July; in fall, let still immature tomatoes finish ripening in a dark, warm place
Tip: All green parts of the plant, including unripe, still-green fruit, contain a toxic alkaloid.

Height:
*5–8 ft
(1.5–2.5 m)*
Harvest Time:
August–October

deciduous tree

Malus domestica

Apple Tree

Family: Rose (Rosaceae)
Origin: Original forms from Western Asia and Europe
Description: Growth depends on whether trained as a bush (dwarf tree) or a spindle tree; flowers in April–May, white to pink; fruit coloration and time of ripeness depend on cultivar
Location: Sunny; somewhat protected
Cultivation: Usually a second small tree is needed as a pollen donor for pollination (not required for "duo apples"); plant so that the thickened grafting spot is about 4 in. (10 cm) above the surface of the soil
Care: Tie to stake; keep evenly damp; use slow-release fertilizer in spring, add more in July if necessary; regular pruning depends on growth habit and age, especially important is keeping the crown thinned out; winter over outdoors with protection
Harvesting: Ready to pick when color is correct for cultivar and when the stem easily loosens when the fruit is twisted
Tip: See also Columnar and Dwarf Apple Trees (→ page 216)

Height:
3–8 ft
(1–2.5 m)
Harvest Time:
August–October

deciduous tree

Malus domestica

Columnar and Dwarf Apple Trees

Family: Rose (Rosaceae)
Origin: Original forms from Western Asia and Europe
Description: Growth: narrow and columnar (columnar or "Ballerina" apple trees, fruit-bearing branches grow directly on the trunk, only about 16 in. (40 cm wide)) or with a compact crown and small trunk (dwarf apple trees, only 3–5 ft (1–1.5 m high)); flowers in April–May, white to pink; fruit color and time of ripeness dependent on cultivar
Location: Sunny; somewhat protected
Cultivation: As for apple tree in general (→ page 215)
Care: As for apple tree in general; however, with columnar trees, trimming is limited to removing annoying lateral shoots and overmature fruiting spurs, while dwarf trees need pruning only every few years; dwarf trees are best wintered over indoors, in a cool, frost-free place
Harvesting: As for apple tree in general (→ page 215)
Species/Cultivars: Columnar apple trees are available only in special cultivars, such as 'Bolero,' 'Polka,' and 'Waltz.' Dwarf apple trees are in some cases small forms of cultivars.

Height:
*8–16 in.
(20–40 cm)*
**Harvest
Time:**
*June–
September*

annual herb

Ocimum basilicum

Basil

Family: Mint (Lamiaceae)
Origin: India, Mediterranean region
Description: Grows bushy and erect; ovate, pointed, helmet-shaped (galeated) glossy green leaves, in some cultivars red or red-brown; small white flowers in July–September
Location: Sunny, also full sun; warm, protected
Cultivation: Grow from seed in late March–April, at 64–68 °F (18–20 °C), light germinator; plant 10 in. (25 cm) apart; put outdoors after mid-May (in areas with harsh weather, late May)
Harvesting: Leaves and young shoots all summer long; most aromatic before the bloom; harvest shoot tips first to promote bushier growth
Tip: Basil can be combined in boxes or containers with balcony tomatoes, lettuces, and zucchini. Red-leaved cultivars are quite decorative.

Height:
*8–24 in.
(20–60 cm)*
**Harvest
Time:**
*May–
September*

*deciduous
semishrub*

Origanum vulgare

Oregano

Other Name: Wild marjoram
Family: Mint (Lamiaceae)
Origin: Southern Europe
Description: Spreading; ovate, aromatic leaves; small labiate
flowers in false umbels, pink, red-violet, or white; bloom
time: July–September
Location: Full sun is best; warm
Cultivation: Grow from seed in March–April, at 72 °F (22 °C),
light germinator; plant in wide tubs, boxes, or bowls; use low-
nutrient substrate (such as propagating soil), mixed with
sand; from early May, place outdoors; protect from late frosts
Care: Water with restraint; no feeding; in October, cut back
and winter over outdoors with winter protection or indoors,
in a frost-free, moderately bright place
Harvesting: Starting in late May, pick leaves and young shoot
tips continuously; most intense aroma during the bloom, also
cut then for drying

Height:
*8–12 in.
(20–30 cm)*
**Harvest
Time:**
*almost year-
round*

*biennial
herb*

Petroselinim crispum var. crispum

Parsley

Family: Carrot (Apiaceae)
Origin: Mediterranean region
Description: Bushy; leaves pinnate, depending on cultivar curly or flat; "shoots" in June/July of the second year, with yellowish umbels on tall stems
Location: Best in light shade, no full sun
Cultivation: Sow seed in mid-March–June directly into planter (germination time: up to five weeks); thin out plants to distance of 4 in. (10 cm); starting in April, place outdoors, on frosty nights cover with tarp or plastic sheeting
Care: Keep evenly damp; feed low dose every two weeks; winter over outdoors with protection or indoors in a very cool, bright place
Harvesting: For seed sown in March, starting in June; otherwise, about eight weeks after sowing; cut leaves off continuously, until shortly before the bloom (in the second year), then no longer usable
Tip: Do not plant parsley with lettuce; it goes well with tomatoes or radishes.

Height:
*10–13 ft
(3–4 m)*
**Harvest
Time:**
*July–
October*

*annual
legume*

Phaseolus coccineus

Scarlet Runner Bean

Family: Legume (Fabaceae)
Origin: Central America, Mexico
Description: Twining plant with large cordate leaves; from June–September, red or white flowers; starting in summer, hairy bean pods, when ripe containing large, mottled, or white seeds
Location: Sun; protected from wind
Cultivation: Grow from seed in mid-April, at 68 °F (20 °C), then plant in May; or, starting in early May, sow directly into planter; best to keep two or three plants in a large pot
Care: Train to grow up wires, twine, or frame; keep damp but never wet; when bloom begins and after pods form, feed with organic or low-nitrogen fertilizer
Harvesting: Pick young, tender pods in July/August; seeds as dry beans when mature in fall
Tip: Pods and seeds of *Phaseolus* beans (including bush and pole beans) are poisonous if eaten raw!

Height:
5–8 ft
(1.5–2.5 m)
Harvest Time:
June– August

deciduous tree

Prunus avium

Sweet Cherry Tree

Family: Rose (Rosaceae)
Origin: Asia Minor
Description: Grows as bush, spindle tree, columnar cherry, or small dwarf tree; white flowers, April–May; usually red, globular to heart-shaped stone fruits
Location: Sunny; warm and protected
Cultivation: Usually not self-fertilizing, second cultivar needed as pollen donor; plant with the thickened graft site above the surface of the soil
Care: Water generously when bearing flowers or fruit, moderately at other times; apply slow-release fertilizer in spring; regular trimming required for bush and spindle tree forms; winter over outdoors with good protection
Harvesting: Time depends on cultivar; pluck cherries with stem or cut off
Tip: Especially in the newer, compact columnar and dwarf forms, the sweet cherry can be grown quite well in a container, with no great pruning effort needed

Height:
*5–8 ft
(1.5–2.5 m)*
**Harvest
Time:**
*August–
October*

*deciduous
tree*

Prunus domestica

Plum

Other Names: European plum, Damson; the species also includes greengage plums and the small Syrian plums
Family: Rose (Rosaceae)
Origin: Asia Minor
Description: Broad-crowned bush or spindle tree; white flowers in April–May; fruit blue, violet, also yellow-green or yellow (greengage, Syrian plums)
Location: Preferably sunny, also partial shade
Cultivation: Best to choose self-fertilizing cultivars on a slow-growing basis; plant with graft site above the surface of the soil
Care: Keep evenly and well dampened; apply slow-release fertilizer in spring, adding more every eight weeks until August; provide support for fruit-bearing branches; after initial pruning of the young bush, only occasional thinning out is needed; winter over outdoors with protection
Harvesting: Time depends on cultivar, can be determined by good coloration; pick thoroughly several times, harvest ripe fruit as soon as possible

Height:
*3–8 ft
(1–2.5 m)*
**Harvest
Time:**
*June–
October*

*deciduous
tree*

Prunus persica
Peach, Nectarine

Family: Rose (Rosaceae)
Origin: China
Description: Growth: as bush (usually lacking central shoot) or as small dwarf tree; pretty, narrow, ovate leaves; light pink flowers, March–April; fruit covered with velvety hair (peach) or smooth-skinned (nectarine)
Location: Sunny; warm and protected; nectarines need more warmth than peaches
Cultivation: Usually self-fertilizing, no pollen-donor cultivar needed; best to plant in spring, with bud union above the surface of the soil
Care: Water copiously when bearing flowers and fruit, moderately otherwise; apply slow-release fertilizer in spring; regular trimming (especially thinning out the crown) is important except for dwarf peaches and nectarines; winter over outdoors with good protection or indoors in a bright, cool place
Harvesting: Time depends on cultivar; ripe when coloration is good; fruit comes off when turned slightly

Height:
3–6.5 ft
(1–2 m)
Harvest Time:
August–October

deciduous tree

Pyrus communis

Pear

Family: Rose (Rosaceae)
Origin: Asia, Europe
Description: Growth habit: bush, spindle tree, or small dwarf pear; white flowers in April–May; fruit, depending on cultivar, green, reddish, or yellowish
Location: Sunny; warm and protected
Cultivation: For fertilization, two or three different cultivars are needed (except with "duo pears"); plant with bud union above soil surface; provide with stake for support; use low-lime, slightly acid substrate
Care: Keep evenly damp; apply slow-release fertilizer in spring, add more in June if needed; needs regular trimming (except dwarf pears), overmature fruit-bearing boughs should be removed or shortened; winter over outdoors with good protection or indoors in a bright, cool place
Harvesting: Time depends on cultivar; fall cultivars are ready to eat two to four weeks after harvest; winter cultivars only after longer storage

Height:
*5–8 ft
(1.5–2 m)*
**Harvest
Time:**
*August–
September*

*deciduous
tree*

Pyrus pyrifolia var. culta
Asian Pear

Other Names: Sand pear, nashi
Family: Rose (Rosaceae)
Origin: East Asia
Description: Grown as bush or spindle tree; white flowers in
April; fruit, depending on cultivar, pear-shaped or apple-
shaped, greenish yellow or yellow, taste pear-like but slightly
acidic and crunchy like apple
Location: Sunny; warm, protected
Cultivation: Needs second Asian pear cultivar or a suitable
pear cultivar as pollen donor; uses low-lime soil; place bud
union above soil surface
Care: Keep evenly damp, use soft water; apply slow-release
fertilizer in spring, add more in June if needed; thin out fruit
to one or two per arrangement if too dense; requires moder-
ate trimming; winter over outdoors with good protection
Harvesting: Not fully ripe until late September; don't leave
ripe fruit hanging on tree for long

Height:
4–6 in.
(10–15 cm)
**Harvest
Time:**
*May–
September*

*tuberous
plant
grown as
annual*

Raphanus sativus var. sativus
Radish

Family: Mustard or cabbage (Brassicaceae)
Origin: Near East and East Asia
Description: Growth: compact, with oval, rough-haired leaves; depending on cultivar, round, oval, or cylindrical tubers, red, reddish white, or white
Location: Sunny, if necessary also partial shade
Cultivation: From late March–August, sow directly in boxes or deep bowls, every few weeks in subsequent sowings; depending on sowing time, choose suitable spring or summer cultivars; thin out young plants to 2–3 in. (6–8 cm) after sprouting, removing the weakest ones altogether
Care: Keep evenly damp; no feeding necessary
Harvesting: Always pick the fattest radishes first, about six weeks after sowing in spring, three to four weeks in summer; tubers harvested too late quickly become woody; fill the "holes" made when harvesting with some soil
Tip: You can sow radishes in sufficiently large planters between tomatoes, lettuces, Swiss chard, or parsley.

Height:
*3–5 ft
(1–1.5 m)*
**Harvest
Time:**
July–August

*deciduous
shrub*

Ribes rubrum

Red Currant

Family: Gooseberry (Grossulariaceae)
Origin: Europe
Description: Growth: broad, bushy with basal main shoots, or trained as a standard (tall or short standards with a trunk height of only 16 in. (40 cm)); inconspicuous flowers in April–May; red berries, in white currants whitish to yellowish berries, in racemes
Location: Prefers sun, but also bears fruit well in partial shade; protected from wind
Cultivation: Self-fertilizing, but a second cultivar improves fructification; plant singly in large pots and slightly acid substrate
Care: Keep evenly and well dampened; apply slow-release fertilizer (low-chloride) in spring, add more in summer if needed; support standard; thin out older shoots after the harvest or in late winter, for tall standards, shorten shoots by one third; winter over outdoors with protection
Harvesting: Best to cut off complete clusters of berries

Height:
16–40 in.
(40–100 cm)
Harvest Time:
March–October

evergreen shrub

Rosmarinus officinalis

Rosemary

Family: Mint (Lamiaceae)
Origin: Mediterranean region
Description: Growth: broad, bushy, densely branching; needle-like, gray-green leaves; delicate blue to violet, more rarely white flowers, in whorls at the shoot tips, from March to June; entire plant has an aromatic scent
Location: Full sun if at all possible; warm, protected
Cultivation: Growing from seed is time-consuming, better to buy young plants; set singly in large pots, care as for Mediterranean plants; propagation from cuttings in August possible
Care: Keep only slightly damp; if necessary, feed in spring after growth begins; winter over in a bright place at 36–46 °F (2–8 °C), put outdoors only after mid-May; repot older plants only rarely
Harvesting: Leaves and shoot tips continually from spring to fall; don't pick too much; in summer, cut off shoots for drying
Tip: Rosemary is also a decorative container plant.

Height:
*1–2 ft
(30–60 cm)*
**Harvest
Time:**
Year-round

*evergreen
semishrub*

S

Salvia officinalis
Sage

Other Names: Common sage, garden sage
Family: Mint (Lamiaceae)
Origin: Southern Europe
Description: Loosely bushy growth habit; longish oval, gray-green, strongly aromatic leaves, in some cultivars colorfully marked or red; light blue-violet labiate flowers in whorls appearing from June to August
Location: Full sun if at all possible; warm, protected
Cultivation: Sow seed directly into planter from April to May; later, prick out young plants to 12 in. (30 cm) or put one or two plants in larger pot; use low-nutrient soil, mixed with some sand; propagation from cuttings in summer possible
Care: Water little; winter over outdoors with protection, or indoors in a bright, frost-free place; cut back by half in spring, then apply low dose of fertilizer
Harvesting: Leaves can be harvested year-round; cut shoots for drying shortly before the bloom
Tip: Cultivars with colorful leaves, such as 'Tricolor,' have ornamental value.

Height:
*1–1.5 ft
(30–40 cm)*
**Harvest
Time:**
*May–
August*

annual herb

Satureja hortensis

Summer Savory

Family: Mint (Lamiaceae)
Origin: Mediterranean region
Description: Growth: bushy, erect, with narrow, leathery leaves; small, delicate pink flowers, July–October
Location: Sunny, also full sun; warm and protected
Cultivation: Sow seeds in April (light germinator), after mid-May plant in pots or balcony boxes; alternatively, sow directly in boxes, thin out to distance of 10 in. (25 cm); subsequent sowings until early June
Care: Use burlap or plastic sheeting to protect from cool early-summer temperatures; keep evenly and slightly damp, apply a low dose of fertilizer once in the growth period
Harvesting: Young shoots all summer long; most aromatic just before and during the bloom; for drying, cut flowering shoots
Species/Cultivars: The perennial winter savory (*S. Montana*) also can be grown in planters and can be wintered over outdoors with some protection.

Height:
*8–16 in.
(20–40 cm)*
**Harvest
Time:**
*April–
October*

*evergreen
semishrub*

Thymus vulgaris

Thyme

Family: Mint (Lamiaceae)
Origin: Southeastern Europe
Description: Cushion-like growth habit; narrow, dark-green leaves; pink to violet flowers from May to October
Location: Best in full sun; warm, protected
Cultivation: Growing from seed difficult, better to buy plants; set out in May, 8 in. (20 cm) apart, or plant singly in pots, in low-nutrient soil mixed with sand; for older plants, propagation from cuttings and by division possible
Care: Keep only slightly damp; winter over indoors, in a bright, cool place, or outdoors with good protection; cut back in spring, then feed sparingly
Harvesting: Cut off young leaves and shoot tips from spring to fall; aroma most intense before the bloom, also the time to cut for drying
Species/Cultivars: Somewhat more sensitive: lemon thyme, *T.* x *citriodorus,* which really has a lemon taste
Tip: Both a pretty ornamental plant and a scented plant

Designing with Plants

The possibilities for decorating balconies and patios with plants are almost as varied as the plants themselves. And since most boxes, tubs, and other containers are planted afresh every year, you can keep trying out new species and cultivars.

Designing Is Fun

The term "designing" calls up associations with aesthetic virtuosity, decorative skill, and sophisticated arrangement. Certainly, all those elements play a role when you design with plants—but there's no need to see it as something beyond your reach. After all, the point is for you to feel comfortable on your balcony or patio, and for the plantings to be enjoyable to look at each and every time.

Tastes differ, as do the sizes and dimensions of "green living rooms," so there are virtually no generally applicable patterns or rules. But some design tricks and basic principles can help you make even more of your plants.

Magnificent Plants at Every Level

To achieve a design that offers both variety and harmony, it can help to visualize the different levels at which plants can be placed.

➤ The **middle level**, usually at eye level when you are seated, often provides an image of the balcony boxes on the railing. On the balcony, at least, the planter boxes with their summer flowers are simultaneously the basis and the framework for your design efforts.

➤ Also usually at **eye level**, container plants and potted woody plants unfold their charms; however, they also require quite a lot of space. On a balcony, they are best used sparingly, preferably as special focal points. On a large patio, however, they can be arranged in groups and constitute the "scaffolding" for the design.

➤ If there is enough room at **ground level**, little groups of small pots and bowls provide an optical "substructure." They can sit directly on the ground or on plant stands and preferably are placed in corners.

An "edging" of blooms can be created with pots on the ground.

The Drama of Plants and Their Surroundings
The plants generally are the stars of the play, but the back-drop (painted wall, railings, floor covering) and props (planters, furnishings, decorative elements) also have a deci-sive effect on their performance. Vividly colored pots or furni-ture, for example, require flower colors that harmonize; yellow and white bloomers are apt to be boring against light-colored walls; and delicate plants can get lost among massive beams.

➤ In the **"air space,"** hang-ing planters and baskets can add marvelous accents, either on the ceiling or on the wall, hung from a pro-jecting mounting.
➤ Last, there is the **vertical aspect**—either for attractive climbing plants, wall planters, or pots and boxes on plant shelving and etageres, which save space and thus expand the room available for placement of plants.
By deliberately taking advantage of these planting levels, you can make the design consistent in struc-ture and varied in effect, even if you limit yourself to only a few plants.

> 1 **Striking spots of color**

> 2 **Hanging planters create accen**

> 3 **Minigardens in pots make a wide variety of combinations possib**

> 4 **Decorative foliage**

Pretty combination of colors 5 >

Attractive Balcony Boxes

Boxes of brightly colored flowers often are the "heart" of a design, not only on a balcony. Effective color combinations (→ page 238) and a well-considered arrangement of the plants will help you create boxes with an extra something.

➤ Boxes that are at least 7–8 in. (18–20 cm), wide and/or deep offer possibilities for very attractive design solutions. Here you can plant in **two rows**. At the back, put tall species like erect geraniums and pelargoniums or fuchsia, leaving the front for smaller, compact species such as ageratum or trailing plants like lobelia. Set the plants in the front row in the "gap" between two of the plants in back; that way, you can maintain the required planting intervals (→ Profiles).

➤ Narrower boxes are planted in **single rows**. Here too, you can use a mixture of erect and hanging plants to add variety. But if the boxes are quite short (31 in. (80 cm) or less), homogeneous plantings can be very pretty. Even with plants of the same species, such as different-colored geraniums, petunias, or Livingstone daisies, you can achieve a satisfying effect.

Some possibilities and variations for combining plants from spring till fall and winter are shown in the examples starting on page 240.

Designing with Colors

In probably every design, it's the colors that appeal most strongly to eye and mind. Through well-aimed use of various **color effects**, you can control the atmosphere created by the overall picture:

EXTRA TIP

Minigarden in Pots
Instead of setting balcony flowers in boxes or bowls, you also can plant them in pots and create arrangements. Thus, you can combine species that would be unlikely to thrive in the same box because of different growth habits or water and nutrient requirements. This will work even on the balcony railing, if you put the pots next to each other inside a planter box.

All in pink: Petunias and nemesia go together here, tone on tone.

➤ Yellow is a warm, cheerful, and happy color.

➤ Red and orange are like signals, and they add warm, lively accents.

➤ Pink, depending on whether red, white, or blue hues are dominant, can be cheerful, tender, and light, or can range from to discreetly elegant to romantic.

➤ Blue has a cool, calming effect, and in some cases is classy and stylish as well.

➤ Violet resembles blue, but is somewhat warmer, depending on the percentage of red.

➤ White has a brightening effect, mediates between contrasting colors, and creates a sense of distance.

➤ Green, the leaf color, should not be underestimated; it has a balancing and calming effect.

Red, blue-violet, and yellow blossoms make a wonderful threesome.

Combining Colors for Effect

There are four time-tested ways of putting flower colors or leaf colors together:

➤ **Color contrasts** can be found in exciting combinations of warm and cool, light and dark, calm and lively colors. Strong contrasts are, for example, orange and blue, yellow and violet, red and green, red and white, light yellow and bright pink.

➤ **Color triad** is a composition in which the colors contrast with each other as strongly as possible. The "classic" combination is red, blue, and yellow. These three components can each be replaced by similar colors (for example, replace red with orange).

➤ **Color blend** uses combinations of similar colors with gentle transitions, such as various tones of yellow and orange.

➤ **Tone on tone** uses combinations of blooms in only one basic color in various shades, ranging, for example, from deep, dark blue to delicate light blue.

EXTRA TIP

Colors, Shapes, and Nuances

If you want to strongly emphasize a certain color, when making your selection, be sure you have enough species with large flowers: They accentuate the chosen tone in an especially striking way. Of course, plants with small, but very numerous blooms also display a lot of color, but they always seem "lighter" and more playful. This applies to hanging plants with their flowing forms as well. Bright pastel shades have an especially airy, romantic effect.

Spring Planting: Goodbye to Winter

As soon as the first spring bloomers open their flowers, balconies and patios become "green living rooms."

Every time you look out the window, a spring planting will bring you special pleasure, since the early blooms are a clear sign that the cold, gloomy days of winter will soon be over and sunny times are approaching. And if you leave the door open on milder days, your nose will be regaled with scents of spring, some delicate, some entrancing.

> **Brilliant yellow and white reveal spring in all its radiance.**

Plants for the Spring Experience

➤ **Bulbous** and **tuberous flowers** make their big entrance in spring. Snowdrops and crocus start in February and are soon followed by the early tulips and narcissus, and then by the splendid hyacinths and ranunculus.

➤ Equally attractive and valuable are the early-blooming **biennials** such as English daisies, forget-me-nots, English wallflowers, and horned violets, as well as bushy asters and bleeding heart. With their rosette-like or bushy growth habit, they can be used in combinations to loosen up the often rather stiff image of bulbs.

➤ Where there is enough room, flowering **potted woody plants** can enrich a spring arrangement. These include, for example, winter jasmine, ornamental cherries (*Prunus species*), and early spiraea (*Spiraea species*), as well as rhododendrons later in the spring.

Planting Tips

➤ Plant the single- or few-stemmed bulbous and tuberous flowers in small groups of at least three, because they often seem rather meager when used singly.

➤ Young plants purchased in spring can be set quite close together. But if you put bulbs or tubers in the ground in fall, you should definitely adhere to the recommended minimum planting distances given in the Plant Profiles, so that the plants can develop properly.

➤ Provide the planters with good drainage, and water with great care, since bulbs and tubers will rot if they stay wet.

PLANTING SUGGESTIONS

Box 32 in. (80 cm) long, 7–8 in. (18–20 cm) wide (as in photo on page 240)

➤ 1 to 2 white ranunculus
➤ 6 yellow narcissus
➤ 3 pinkish white tulips
➤ 1 yellow and 1 white hornet violet
➤ 1 to 2 pink or blue forget-me-nots

Bowl 16 in. (40 cm) in diameter

➤ 15 crocuses in mixed colors
➤ 9 yellow early-blooming narcissus
➤ 9 red early tulips

Bowl 12 in. (30 cm) in diameter

➤ 9 white tulips
➤ 4 blue hyacinths
➤ 5 yellow horned violets

Box 40 in. (100 cm) long, 8 in. (20 cm) wide

➤ 12 yellow narcissus
➤ 2 red-leaved bergenias
➤ 5 blue horned violets

Sunny Summer Splendor

Wherever the sun shines down almost all day long, you really have the agony of choice. Most summer flowers like the sun, as do the majority of the container plants, but even a sunny location has its shady sides. Popular beauties such as fuchsias, begonias, and impatiens are less apt to flourish here. And even many summer bloomers are just as affected by the heat as the owners of balconies and patios. An awning or a parasol, therefore, is a worthwhile acquisition. Only downright sun-lovers like gazanias, African daisies, Livingstone daisies, and moss rose are scarcely bothered by blazing sun. Their warm colors seem to collect the sunlight. Because the flowers usually stay closed on gloomy days, however, don't place all your money on such sun specialists.

Charming Balcony Boxes

Our planting suggestion is based on species that won't fail you completely, even in a rainy summer. The decidedly large box was used here for three rows of plantings

Large boxes are the best places for such a luxuriant display to develop.

(see also page 237). Independently of that, the box demonstrates a proven principle of planting: **symmetry**. The left and right sides of the box are almost identical. And although the petunias have very "strong" partners here, they still remain the focal point. This role can be played both by large plants with striking blooms and by opulent hanging plants. In a symmetrical arrangement, such indicator plants form the center or are placed left and right of the center.

An **asymmetrical** design, with the focal point moved to one side, can also be effective. The second planting idea described at right takes a modest step in that direction. The structure is otherwise symmetrical, but on the left edge of the box a blue marguerite rises up, while on the right a Swan River daisy cascades downward.

Box 48 in. (120 cm) long, 8.5 in. (22 cm) wide, planted in three rows (as in photo on page 242)

➤ 1 erect pink petunia
➤ 2 tall blue-violet lobelias
➤ 2 Apache beggarticks
➤ 3 deep pink hanging verbenas
➤ 1 white and 2 pale pink hanging petunias

Tip: For an even more brightly colored version, you can replace the pink and white petunias with red cultivars.

Box 40 in. (100 cm) long, 8 in. (20 cm) wide, planted in two rows

➤ 1 deep blue nemesia, for center back
➤ 2 velvet-red erect geraniums, left and right of the nemesia
➤ 1 blue marguerite, left back
➤ 1 blue Swan River daisy
➤ 2 yellow creeping zinnias, left and right front
➤ 1 ground morning glory, center front

Summer in Partial Shade

Balconies and patios with partial shade definitely have their advantages. The partial shade makes being outside in the heat of high summer more pleasant, and the plants don't need to be watered quite so often.

Partial Shade—the Subtle Differences

From light to heavy shade, from occasional shade in the morning to shade at midday or in the late afternoon—shade has a great many nuances, which can have different effects on plant growth and bloom. In

> **Snapdragons and fuchsias add color to locations with partial shade.**

the final analysis, you must simply experiment to see what thrives in your own "green living room." Where even the very partial-shade-tolerant geraniums and petunias will no longer bloom satisfactorily, fuchsias, begonias, and impatiens offer attractive alternatives. Fuchsias play a major role in our planting suggestion as well, with brilliant yellow snapdragons as a foil, supported by dainty wax begonias.

Dapper Woody Plants in Pots

Not only fuchsias and other partial-shade varieties but also a number of very pretty potted woody plants reveal their special forte in partial shade—first and foremost are rhododendrons and hydrangeas, which are available in very compact forms. Evergreens such as boxwood or Japanese skimmia tolerate even more shade. Of the container plants, camellia and Paraguay nightshade, for example, bloom especially well in partially-

Hydrangeas bloom especially well in light shade.

PLANTING SUGGESTIONS

Box 40 in (100 cm) long, 7–8 in. (18–20 cm) wide, planted in two rows (as in photo on page 244)

➤ 2 red hanging fuchsias
➤ 2 yellow snapdragons
➤ 1 white and 1 pink wax begonia

Box 32 in. (80 cm long), 8 in. (18 cm) wide, planted in one row

➤ 1 red-violet impatiens for the center
➤ 2 blue-violet Carpathian bellflowers, right and left of the impatiens
➤ 2 silver-leaved spotted dead nettles (*Lamium maculatum*), trailing, for the sides of the box

Potted arrangement, various pots and tubs

➤ 1 white hydrangea
➤ 1 red fuchsia standard, underplanted with white-mottled ivy
➤ 1 small bay tree
➤ 2 hostas, one blue-leaved, one with white-edged leaves

shaded locations, and even angel's trumpet often finds partial shade quite agreeable.

Pleasures in the Shade

Not all shade is the same, as is implied in the discussion of partial shade (→ pages 245/246), and there is definitely no reason to give up hope (→ Tip in box on page 11). And you can even improve dark locations a bit by giving preference to light-colored paints, furnishings, and the like. That not only brightens things visually but also slightly increases the amount of light available to the plants.

(→ pages 245/246)... (→ Tip in box on page 11).

PLANTING SUGGESTIONS

Potted arrangement, various planters
➤ 1 Japanese aucuba with yellow-green leaves
➤ 1 red-blooming fuchsia standard
➤ 2 small boxwood trees
➤ 1 box with red-leaved bergenias and white-blooming impatiens
➤ several ferns (such as common male fern, *Dryopteris filix-mas*)

Tuberous begonias and impatiens will illuminate shady locations.

PLANTING SUGGESTIONS

Deep bowl, 24 in. (60 cm) in diameter (as in photo on page 246)

➤ 1 red and 2 bright pink impatiens

➤ 4 tuberous begonias: 2 yellow, 1 red-orange, and 1 white

➤ 3 small ivy plants with white-green markings

Potted arrangement, various planters

➤ 3 dwarf astilbes: 2 red and 1 white with blue-green leaves

➤ 1 Japanese hosta

➤ in a box: white bellflowers, common bugle variegated in white (*Ajuga reptans*)

Proven Bloomers in Shade

Even in heavier shade, the popular trio of fuchsias, impatiens, and tuberous begonias often can work little floral miracles. Of course, you need to be alert and ask questions when purchasing, to keep from bringing home special sun-tolerant cultivars of these flowers. Hydrangeas and other beauties listed in the partial-shade section will in some cases still bloom quite satisfactorily in shade.

Shade Experts

Some herbaceous perennials are true shade artists. In particular, astilbe, hosta, and bergenia have proven their worth in pot culture, and don't forget ferns and ivy, which are good companions

> **Astilbe and hosta are pretty, dependable choices for shady locations.**

for such plants. Some very decorative ornamental foliage plants, too, are espe-

> **Fall plantings delight the eye with a special charm of their own.**

cially good in shade, including aucuba, bay laurel, boxwood, cherry laurel, and sago palm.

Autumn and Winter Delights

Fall and winter plantings do more than make it easier to say goodbye to summer on the balcony. Not only can the sight of them cheer you on gloomy days late in the year, but they also have their own flair and are far more than a mere substitute for summer's lush beauty.

➤ For the first **fall plantings** in September, you need to keep ready a few additional boxes, pots, and bowls because many summer flowers will keep on blooming right up until the first frosts. In contrast to them, however, the fall bloomers now are just coming into their own, including late-planted fall chrysanthemums, bushy asters, stonecrop, heather, and Scotch heather. You can combine them with a host of lovely foliage plants, not just dependable partners like dusty miller and ivy. In recent years, garden centers have greatly expanded their offerings, adding plants with reddish, silvery, bluish, or variegated leaves that often adorn your planters well into winter.

➤ **Winter adornments** include the little coniferous and deciduous woody plants, which can also be combined in balcony boxes when they are young. If they haven't already done so, the evergreen dwarf woody plants will take over the show. Yellow- and blue-needled conifers add new color to the spectacle, as do ornamental fruit, as in the case with Japanese skimmia and prickly heath. Winter heath, some forms of Scotch heather, the unusual Christmas rose, or a winter jasmine in a tub will bloom.

SUGGESTIONS

Fall
Bowl 24 in. (60 cm) in diam. (photo-page 248)
➤ 4 small stonecrop plants (*Sedum* hybrids)
➤ 1 prickly heath (*Gaultheria mucronata*)
➤ 2 spotted dead nettles (*Lamium maculatum*) with white mottled leaves
➤ 1 common bugle with variegated foliage (*Ajuga reptans*)
➤ 1 Japanese sweetflag (*Acorus gramineus*)

Winter
Box 24–32 in. (60–80 cm) long, 7–8 in. (18–20 cm) wide (photo-page 249)

➤ 1 dwarf pine (such as *Pinus mugo* 'Mops')
➤ 2 pink winter heath plants
➤ 1 ivy plant with white-green markings

Box 32 in. (80 cm) long, 7 in. (18 cm) wide

➤ winter heath: 1 white, 1 pink, 1 red, in center
➤ 1 yellow Japanese false cypress (*Chamaecyparis pisifera* 'Plumosa aurea'), left
➤ 1 blue dwarf juniper (*Juniperus squamata* 'Blue Star'), right

Plant Index

The page numbers in **bold** refer to photographs.